AMERICAN INDIAN POPULATION RECOVERY

IN THE TWENTIETH CENTURY

AMERICAN

INDIAN

POPULATION

RECOVERY

IN THE

TWENTIETH

CENTURY

Nancy Shoemaker

*University of
New Mexico Press
Albuquerque*

First paperbound printing, 2000

Library of Congress Cataloging-in-Publication Data

Shoemaker, Nancy, 1958–

    American Indian population recovery in the

    Twentieth Century / Nancy Shoemaker.—1st ed.

        p.   cm.

    Originally presented as the author's thesis

    (University of Minnesota).

    Includes bibliographical references (p.) and index.

    ISBN 0-8263-1919-X   ISBN 0-8263-2289-1

    1. Indians of North America—Population. I. Title.

E98.P76S56   1999

304.6'08997—dc21   98-45402

                                   CIP

CONTENTS

FIGURES

TABLES

Europeans settlement of the Americas initiated a devastating decline in the native population. In the area now lying within the United States, the American Indian population dropped from an estimated several million people to fewer than 250,000 in 1900. Except for a slight decrease in 1920, the Indian population has rapidly increased in the twentieth century, until now there are nearly two million Indians in the United States.

Most research in American Indian historical demography has focused on the catastrophic population loss that resulted from European contact. We know considerably less about the Indian population recovery, the phenomenal growth of the Indian population since 1900. And yet, the population recovery is one of the most important events in American Indian history, since it has once and for all vanquished the myth of the Vanishing Indian and laid the foundation for an American Indian political and cultural revitalization.

Recently, scholars have paid increased attention to Indian demography in the twentieth century. C. Matthew Snipp's *American Indians: The First of This Land*, an analysis of the 1980 U.S. census, is the most thorough study of American Indian families and demographic patterns to date. Russell Thornton's survey of Indian population history since 1492, *American Indian Holocaust and Survival*, has a chapter on the population recovery, and a few other chapters address twentieth-century population issues. There are also several books on the demographic history of particular tribes, including Stephen Kunitz's *Dis-*

ease Change and the Role of Medicine: The Navajo Experience and Russell Thornton's *The Cherokees: A Population History.*

My research started with this literature but examines more directly how and why American Indians recovered from population loss. The past few decades of research into their population decline have documented in great detail its causes and its social, cultural, and economic consequences. But what caused the reversal of the Indian population from dwindling to thriving? Why in the twentieth century has the Indian population grown so rapidly? And finally, now that the Indian population approaches numerical levels equivalent in size to some 1492 estimates, what are the social, cultural, and economic implications of the family and demographic patterns fueling the recovery?

Most of the subsequent analysis treats 1900, the low point or nadir of the Indian population, as a focal point. After an introductory chapter giving an overview of Indian historical demography, three chapters center on a comparison of five different Indian groups: the Seneca Nation in New York State, the Oklahoma Cherokees, the Red Lake Ojibways in Minnesota, the Yakamas in Washington State, and the Navajos in the Southwest.

Specifically, chapter 2, a collection of population histories, contrasts the timing and pace of demographic decline and recovery for these five tribes. Chapter 3 is a demographic analysis of individual-level federal census data for 1900. And chapter 4 shows how cultural and economic differences between Indian groups at the turn of the century explain why some tribes recovered from population loss more readily than others.

In Chapter 5, an analysis of individual-level federal census data for Indians nationwide from 1940 to 1980 assesses the post-recovery situation. The Indian population in the twentieth century did more than simply recover from a dramatic decline. American Indians became one of the fastest growing subgroups of the U.S. population, and this rapid growth has far-reaching political and social implications for Indians and for American society in general.

Throughout the book, my main source of information on Indian demographic and family patterns is individual-level census data. So that readers can place the experience of Indians in a broader context, I also regularly compare their demographic patterns to those of whites and blacks in the United States. For the comparison of five tribes, I collected five data sets from the manuscript forms of the 1900 federal census. The *1900 U.S. Census Public Use Sample* provided the data for whites and blacks. Chapter 5, which covers the period from 1940 through 1980, is based on analysis of *U.S. Census Public Use (Microdata) Samples* for Indians, whites, and blacks. Readers may wish to start with the appendix, which describes the 1900 and 1940–80 data and discusses issues of data reliability.

At one point I attempted to bring the study up to 1990, but the massive undercounting in the 1990 census and the Census Bureau's later, repeated recalls of the *1990 Public Use Sample* convinced me that I would be better off ending the study with what many analysts consider the Census Bureau's best products: the 1980 census and the *Public Use Sample* drawn from it.

There are many people who helped me when this project started as a dissertation. First and foremost, I thank Russell Menard and Steven Ruggles. As my adviser at the University of Minnesota, Rus read the manuscript many times, each time offering suggestions that ultimately led me to insights and conclusions I wish I had seen from the beginning. And Steve taught me almost everything I know about quantitative methods. Also, Russell Thornton and Melissa Meyer offered crucial advice during the early stages as I formulated the project. I first learned about the significance of the Indian population recovery in Russ Thornton's course in American Indian population history. And Melissa pointed out the utility of census data as a resource for American Indian social history. I also want to thank Frederick Hoxie, who brought me in to work on the American Indian Family History Project at the Newberry Library. The opportunity to work on a project similar to my dissertation research but based on the experiences of five other Indian tribes (Hopi, White Earth Ojibway, Creek, Crow, and Colville) added immeasurably to my skills and understanding of the problems and possibilities in using census data for Indian history.

Other people helped by offering technical assistance, by reading a chapter or chapters, by serving on graduate committees when I first proposed and then later defended the dissertation, or by encouraging me to pursue the revisions and turn the dissertation into a book: Liz Faue, Ron Goeken, Steve Gross, John Howe, Sheila Johansson, Miriam King, Tom King, Janet Lindman, Peggy Marini, Elaine Tyler May, Bob McCaa, Jean O'Brien, Stuart Schwartz, Janet Spector, Jeff Stewart, Ed Tebbenhoff, Ruth Townsend, and Eileen Walsh. A fellowship from the University of Minnesota Graduate School supported a year's worth of research and writing. A Women and Minority Mentoring Grant from the University of Wisconsin-Eau Claire provided support for the revisions.

CHAPTER ONE

AN OVERVIEW OF AMERICAN INDIAN DEMOGRAPHIC HISTORY

M ost of the literature in American Indian historical demography has focused on a single question: What was the native population of the Americas in 1492? Although precontact population size has been widely researched, there is no consensus in sight. Estimates for pre-Columbian North and South America range from 8 million to 112 million. The growing gap between low and high estimates makes one wonder about the reliability of any estimate. The nature of the evidence raises further doubts. Archaeological methods, such as analysis of skeletal remains and models of an area's carrying capacity, rest on shaky assumptions. Written records are similarly problematic since the earliest documented population statistics were fragmentary and biased to support particular goals. In addition, Old World diseases, now recognized as the major cause of native depopulation, frequently struck Indian communities before actual European contact and thus before European observers could record their fragmentary and biased notes on native population size. Research continues on this issue, however, for not knowing the size of the population in 1492 limits our ability to gauge the extent of the decline brought on by European contact.[1]

We may never know exactly what the demographic consequences of European conquest were, but everyone agrees that they were severe. In both North and South America, the native population declined as the influx of Europeans steadily increased. Some native groups were entirely wiped out by smallpox and warfare. Others survived through migration and political consolidation. And still others, though equally vulnerable to the onslaught of new diseases, expanded in influence and population by building connections to the emerging European-dominated global economy. As tribes and regions long exposed to Euro-Americans began to recover from population loss, Euro-Americans encroached on interior tribes, bringing disease and dislocation with them.[2]

In much of Latin America, the native population began recovering from the first extreme population losses about 150 years after initial contact. Densely settled areas with intense European intervention, such as Central Mexico and Peru, seem to have begun their recoveries around 1650. However, Indians living in the interior of Brazil probably did not experience significant population loss and subsequent recovery until the eighteenth and nineteenth centuries. And the indigenous population of Hispaniola never recovered, since within thirty or forty years of European contact, Hispaniola's native population had almost completely died out.[3]

In North America, the process of European contact and depopulation similarly took several centuries and obscures what the aboriginal, precontact population was. Estimates for the pre-Columbian population residing in the area north of Mexico, variously defined as north of the Rio Grande or north of Mesoamerica, range from Alfred Kroeber's 1939 estimate of 900,000 to Henry Dobyns's more recent estimate of 18 million. Kroeber started with James Mooney's research notes, published posthumously in 1928, and then adjusted Mooney's figures for California. Whereas Mooney had estimated 1.15 million Indians north of the Rio Grande at the time of contact, Kroeber substituted lower figures for California and speculated that with further research Mooney's estimate would "ultimately shrink to around 900,000."[4] For both Mooney and Kroeber, the time of contact stretched across several centuries, depending on the region, and so their estimates are more of a composite figure than an actual figure capturing population size at a particular point in time. In a 1966 publication, based on research in the historical record and on the methods of such population estimators as Sherburne Cook, Henry Dobyns determined that the population of various Indian groups had declined by about 20 or 25 to one. He then took the number of Indians reported as living in the United States and Canada in 1930, which he asserted was the nadir of the Indian population, and multiplied it by 20 and by 25, the result being 9.8 to 12.25 million. In his 1983 book *Their Number Become Thinned*, Dobyns nearly doubled his earlier estimate and proposed a new estimate of 18 million.[5]

Although Dobyns persuaded some readers, the trend among other estimators has been for moderation. Several of these more moderate estimates challenged Dobyns on some points but accepted as feasible the method of "depopulation ratios." Harold Driver proposed a lower estimate by amending Dobyns's original numbers while retaining the "multiplier × nadir = estimate" formula. Using the 1890 census as the nadir point for Indians in the United States and a multiplier of 10 or 5, depending on the region, Driver arrived at 3.5 million for North America, which he concluded "seems more plausible than a larger number."[6] Thornton and Marsh-Thornton further revised Dobyns's estimates by using his multipliers but with a lower nadir, which led to a total of 7.7 to 9.6 million. Thornton later wrote that "the most reasonable estimate" for North America is 7 million or more Indians, based on Dobyns's depopulation ratios and revised nadirs for Canada and for the United States.[7]

The other recent scholar to propose estimates is Douglas Ubelaker. Like Kroeber, Ubelaker started with Mooney's research and methods but revised Mooney's figures and arrived at a higher number. Ubelaker collated the population estimates proffered by contributors to the Smithsonian's *Handbook of North American Indians*, a multivolume collection of essays organized by region and tribe, and eventually arrived at an estimate of 1.9 million Indians in North America in 1500.[8]

Most estimators consider Kroeber's low estimate too low and Dobyns' high estimates, whether 12 million or 18 million, much too high. The majority of estimates fall in the range of 2 to 7 million. For the contiguous United States, the estimates fall more within the range of about one to 5.5 million. Whatever the population of North America in 1492, the subsequent population decline was catastrophic. By 1900, the number of Indians in the United States reached a low point of 237,000.

Table 1.1 lists the official figures reported by the U.S. Census Bureau for the Indian population from 1850 to 1990 and documents the tail end of the decline and the accelerating pace of the recovery. At first the U.S. Constitution excluded most Indians, called "Indians Not Taxed," from census enumeration. Not until 1890 were all Indians in the United States enumerated in the federal census, which means that Indian population totals during the decline derive largely from estimates provided by the Bureau (or Office) of Indian Affairs. By 1850, boundary claims in North America had settled to the current national boundaries, and in making estimates of the Indian population, the U.S. government was probably able to obtain fairly reliable reports from its Indian agents. However, Indian population totals—whether estimates, actual census counts, or totals from Indian Affairs annuity lists—were subject to misreporting, both undercount and overcount. The figures in table 1.1 are deceptively precise and should instead be considered rough estimates.

Although the Indian population in the United States did not begin recovering from population loss until after 1900, the pattern of recovery was similar to that in Latin America: regions and tribes experienced demographic loss and demographic recovery at different times and at different rates. The overall population recovery for Indians in the United States did not begin until 1900 because it

TABLE 1.1

Native American Population
in the United States, 1850–1990

Year	Total (Includes Alaska Natives Beginning in 1960)	Year	Total (Includes Alaska Natives Beginning in 1960)
1850	400,764	1930	332,397
1860	339,421	1940	333,969
1870	313,712	1950	343,410
1880	306,543	1960	551,669
1890	248,253	1970	827,268
1900	237,196	1980	1,420,400
1910	265,683	1990	1,959,234
1920	244,437		

Note: In 1950, when Alaska Natives and the contiguous U.S. Indian population were still being tabulated separately, the total Alaska Native population was 33,863, making the total native population 377,273.

Sources: U.S. Census Office, *Indians Taxed and Indians Not Taxed in the United States (except Alaska) at the Eleventh Census: 1890* (Washington, D.C.: GPO, 1894), 5; Edna Lee Paisano, Bureau of the Census, to the author, 23 February 1994.

took Euro-Americans several centuries to conquer the entire continent. Severe smallpox epidemics and warfare between neighboring Indian tribes and between the U.S. military and Indians persisted through the nineteenth century. Also, the preferred U.S. policy of pushing Indians away from white settlement and removing them to interior reservations made it more difficult for Indian communities to establish social and economic stability.[9]

Table 1.1 shows how the Indian population has increased in the twentieth century. Except for a drop in 1920, the Indian population grew rapidly after reaching nadir in 1900. There are two reasons for the decline in 1920. The 1918–19 global influenza epidemic affected Indians as much, if not more, than other Americans, and budgetary constraints on the 1920 census collection meant that the Census Bureau took no special care to enumerate Indians as it had with the 1890 through 1910 censuses and the 1930 census. From 1950 to 1990 the Indian population grew more than fourfold, an increase which in demographic terms could be called "unnatural." In every census year since 1960, considerably more people across age groups have reported their race as Indian. Since immigration for American Indians is negligible, the reasons for recent Indian population growth must be changes in racial definitions, census procedures, and, most importantly, ethnic identity.

The determination of who is "Indian" has a long history of ambiguity. The most common standard applied today is some degree of "Indian blood." Most government programs and services use one-quarter "Indian blood" to judge eligibility, and many Indian tribes have blood-quantum requirements for tribal enrollment. Before 1960 census enumerators classified race based on observation. When in doubt, the enumerator could fall back on a list of criteria: enrollment in a tribe or at an agency, community recognition as Indian, and the "degree of Indian blood." Individuals of mixed parentage were to be classified as the race of the nonwhite parent. Since 1960 the Census Bureau has employed self-identification as the sole criterion: anyone who says they are Indian is Indian.[10]

When the Census Bureau introduced self-identification for race in 1960, many people who in previous censuses had been classified as white or black now said they were Indian. Before 1960 Indians were undercounted in the census because enumerators used physical appearance and residence as the basis for racial classification. A government study matching infant birth records with the 1950 census found that the race given for whites and blacks nearly always matched, but 15 percent of those who were Indian according to the birth records were listed as white in the census.[11] The surge in the Indian population in 1960 is thus partly a rebound from earlier undercounting of people who self-identified as Indian, but the 1970, 1980, and 1990 censuses also resulted in "unnatural" leaps in the Indian population, which must reflect changes in ethnic identity.[12] Contemporary movements for cultural pluralism and ethnic pride have made it socially acceptable for more people to identify as Indian, and children of racially intermarried couples may also be more likely to identify as Indian than previously. Simultaneously, Indian intermarriage with non-Indians has increased. Nearly half of the children ages ten and under who were listed as Indian in the 1980 census had one non-Indian parent.[13] The high rates of intermarriage have created more people of Indian descent with the option to decide their primary racial identity. And most forms, including census forms, force people to choose only one race.

For demographic analysis it would be useful to know which of the people who now identify as Indian were classified as Indian in earlier censuses so that we could distinguish between behavioral changes and compositional changes. Unfortunately, the U.S. Census Bureau does not ask questions such as "What race did you say you were ten years ago?" Census analysts Passel and Berman devised a methodology to deal with the changes in Indian identity, but their approach mistakenly conceives of this problem as a flaw in the data. They classified Indians into two categories based on residence in either all states within the United States or particular "Indian States." "Indian States" are states with three thousand or more Indians in the 1950 census, excluding California, where there have been massive increases in the number of people identifying as Indian. This method ignores the issue of migration. The period from 1950 to 1980 has seen large migrations of Indian people from the reservations to cities and other states, many to California.[14]

Moreover, Passel and Berman's method does not create better quality data but instead privileges a particular definition of "Indian" over others. One hidden implication in their method is that enumerator observation is a more accurate way to determine race. Historically, race has been connected to skin color, which is something someone else observes about you and assigns to you. Now that race is commonly conceptualized as a socially constructed category and a matter of identity, the Census Bureau has simply changed with the times by allowing individuals to say what race they are. And self-identification of race is surely preferable to enumerator observation.

The change in Indian identity is a social phenomenon that we should want our data to reflect, not avoid. In an ideal world social scientists would like their populations to be stable, but in the real world they never are. Most of the populations that historical demographers study are changing in composition. The population of the United States grew in size and became more ethnically diverse throughout the nineteenth and early twentieth centuries because of immigration, and yet much of the research on the American fertility decline measures changes over time in a population defined as native-born whites. While separate studies might examine how immigration affected the American fertility decline, establishing the parameters of fertility change for the entire American population, compositional changes and all, is important as well. The same logic should apply to studying changes in the Indian population.

There are, however, some valid concerns that the changes in identity and census enumeration procedures muddle demographic analysis and could mislead policymakers. Matthew Snipp demonstrated the potential problems by analyzing the two separate questions on race and ancestry in the 1980 census. He found that only 947,500 people said they were "Indian" in response to the race question and also wrote "Indian" in response to the ancestry question, whereas 5.5 million people claimed Indian ancestry but identified their race as non-Indian. Because 29 percent of the people identifying as racially Indian lived below the poverty line in 1980—compared to 15 percent of non-Indian people with some Indian ancestry—the ambiguous boundary between racial and ethnic identity can have serious policy implications. Snipp's research showed that there is a large pool of people, mostly white, who are on the margins of an Indian identity. We can assume that the people who have recently changed their ethnic

FIGURE 1.1

American Indian Population, 1900–1980

Population (in 1000s) (y–Logarithmic Scale)

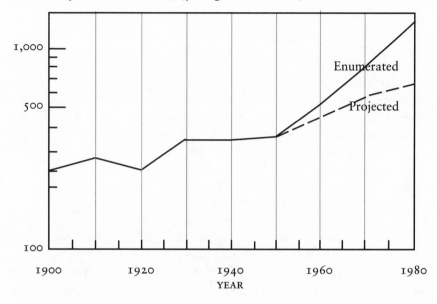

YEAR

identity have come from this pool of people. Their migration into the Indian race has changed the demographic characteristics of the Indian population by making Indians appear to be more like whites. For the rest of his analysis of Indian data from the 1980 census, Snipp defined the Indian population as those people who said they were Indian in response to the question on race.[15] That is also the variable I have used in collecting samples of the Indian population from the census.

Concern about how changes in identity have affected the size of the Indian population should not overwhelm researchers and lead them to ignore the demographic causes of population growth.[16] Natural increase was still an important factor in the great surges in the Indian population that began in 1960. Figure 1.1 shows this by giving two trajectories of population growth, the actual population figures for Indians from 1900 to 1980 (from table 1.1) and estimated figures derived from a population projection using the 1950 census as a base with births added and deaths subtracted according to vital rates for Indians from 1960 to 1980.[17] Even without the changes in census procedures and identity, the Indian population in the postwar period had birth and death rates favoring rapid population growth. My analysis of 1940–80 Indian demography in chapter 5 does not adjust for compositional changes, but I will frequently point out how the changing composition of the Indian population influenced the direction of change in demographic and social patterns.[18]

Population growth can have at most only three causes: fertility, mortality, and migration. Shifts in racial identity constitute a kind of migration because people "migrate" into a different race category, but geographic migration cannot have had much of an impact since American Indians are, by any definition, indigenous to the Americas. Mortality and fertility were the essential components of Indian population growth and have also been the favored subjects of study among demographers, especially those seeking to understand the demographic transition. Most industrialized nations experienced a demographic transition beginning in the nineteenth century as mortality and fertility levels dramatically declined. Indians also experienced this demographic transition, but in the twentieth century and concurrent with renewed growth of the Indian population.

Changes in Indian mortality lie behind both the decline and the recovery of the Indian population. The wealth of research into the devastating impact of Old World diseases on New World people sometimes gives the impression that before European contact the Americas were a paradise of good health and high life expectancies. But the evidence, what there is, suggests that life expectancy at birth was about the same or lower than life-expectancy rates in western Europe in the fifteenth century. Before European contact, Indian life expectancy at birth, based on analysis of skeletal remains, is estimated to have been about twenty-three years, give or take five years.[19] The introduction of European diseases led to higher mortality and population decline. Growing immunity to those diseases, a rising standard of living, medical innovations (vaccinations for smallpox and other diseases, antibiotics, germ theory, and treatments for tuberculosis that worked) were all crucial steps to increasing life expectancy for American Indians and the world's population generally.

Information on Indian mortality is meager, however, even for the twentieth century. Vital statistics, usually the primary means to estimate life expectancy, have always been inadequately kept for the Indian population. At the turn of the century, the Bureau of Indian Affairs asked agents stationed at Indian reservations throughout the country to collect birth and death records, but they either claimed complete inability to collect such information or admitted that the figures they provided were wildly unreliable guesswork. Few Indians had incentives to report births and deaths, and most Indians did not give birth or die in hospitals. The situation did not change significantly until 1955, when the U.S. Public Health Service took over responsibility for Indian health from the Bureau of Indian Affairs. Today, the Indian Health Service provides most of what we know about Indian mortality and health statistics.[20]

TABLE 1.2

Life Expectancy at Birth, 1940–1980

			Difference in Years	
			Indian- White	Black- White
	Indians	Whites	Blacks	
1940	51.0	64.2	53.1	13.2	11.1
1950	60.0	69.1	60.8	9.1	8.3
1960	61.7	70.6	63.6	8.9	7.0
1970	65.1	71.7	64.1	6.6	7.6
1980	71.1	74.4	68.1	3.3	6.3

Note: For 1940–1960, the only available figures are for blacks and other nonwhite races; in 1970 and 1980, black life expectancy at birth was about a year lower than that for blacks and others.

Sources: Everett R. Rhoades, Anthony J. D'Angelo, and Ward B. Hurlburt, "The Indian Health Service Record of Achievement," *Public Health Reports* 102 (July–August 1987), 357; U.S. Census Bureau, *Historical Statistics of the United States*, pt. 1 (Washington, D.C.: GPO, 1975), 55; U.S. Census Bureau, *Statistical Abstract of the United States, 1988* (Washington, D.C.: GPO, 1988), 70.

Despite the problem of obtaining accurate mortality figures for Indians, rough estimates of life expectancy are available. Data from the 1900 census suggest that mortality for Indians in the early twentieth century was considerably higher than among other Americans. Indian life expectancy at birth ranged from twenty to thirty-five years, while other Americans had a life expectancy at birth of almost fifty years. Indian life expectancy began to improve in the 1930s with the declining incidence of tuberculosis, and as the federal government overhauled reservation health programs. The postwar period showed even more rapid improvements.[21] Since 1940 Indian life-expectancy rates have progressively moved closer to the U.S. average. Table 1.2, reprinted from an Indian Health Service report, gives life expectancies at birth for Indians and U.S. whites from 1940 to 1980. Life-expectancy figures for blacks, obtained from other sources, are also listed. In the twentieth century Indian mortality levels have declined considerably. In 1940 Indian life expectancy was thirteen years lower than that for whites, but by 1980 it was only three years lower. The gap between white and black life expectancy has also become smaller; however, Indian life expectancy is now higher than that for blacks.

On the surface, these mortality statistics look like good news for Indians and, as the Indian Health Service is always quick to point out, good news for the

Indian Health Service. However, the rapid rise in life expectancy for Indians, more than any other quantitative measure presented in this book, is confounded by the changes in racial identity. Parents might identify a child's race at birth, or whoever fills out the birth certificate might determine race by the race of parents and in accord with guidelines set by the National Center for Health Statistics. At death someone else determines race. Thus all of the crucial documents for population data in the United States—birth records, death records, and censuses—use different methods for determining race, which creates at least three sources for bias.

First there is the previously discussed problem of how those people who have recently become Indian probably have demographic characteristics more similar to whites. In part, Indian life-expectancy rates have approached those for whites because more whites have moved into the group of people identifying their race as Indian. A second and related source for bias in Indian mortality rates comes from the combined use of vital statistics data with census data. The census is often used as the denominator in calculating death and birth rates. Self-identification of race accounts for much of the surge in the Indian census population since 1970 but has had less of an immediate impact on vital statistics data. Passel and Berman observed some changes in ethnic identity being captured by vital statistics data by 1980, but it was clearly much easier for people to mark the Indian box on the census form than for their doctors or funeral directors to realize they were Indian.[22] Thus the denominator for calculating death rates would be inflated. Whether birth records or census data served as the source of information on the base population, the number of deaths would be understated and life expectancy would be consequently overstated.[23]

Third, death and birth records might not be in agreement about the race of an individual. A recent study by Kennedy and Deapen examined this issue as they tried to figure out why Indian infant mortality in Oklahoma was so low. The average mortality rate for Indian infants for the years 1975 to 1988 was 8.9 deaths per 1,000 live births, compared to 12.1 for all races in Oklahoma and 11.75 for whites. By comparing the race of individuals given on the birth and death records, Kennedy and Deapen found that "infants born Indian had a 28 percent chance of being misclassified as another race (usually white) on the death certificate. Infants born white or black had less than a 1 percent chance of being misclassified."[24] Their revised calculation of the Indian infant mortality rate was 16.7 deaths per 1,000 births.

Indian mortality has declined since World War II, but the life-expectancy figures are excessively optimistic. Research into Indian health, mortality, and crime has revealed high rates of homicide and suicide, and unusually high rates of accidental death, diabetes, and fetal alcohol syndrome. These patterns are discernible in both reservation and urban communities but are correlated with poverty and are most severe on the poorest Indian reservations.[25]

As with mortality, data limitations prevent analyzing fertility before the twentieth century. European observers, from the moment they stepped onto American shores, nearly always remarked upon how few children Indian women bore.[26] Although not systematic, the consistency of their remarks suggests that Indian fertility in the sixteenth through nineteenth centuries was lower than that for their Euro-American contemporaries. Although low by contemporary standards, by today's standards Indian fertility was high and probably remained high throughout the nineteenth century.

Fertility for white women in the United States started to decline in the early nineteenth century. The fertility decline for blacks began in the late nineteenth century.[27] Since comparable nineteenth-century information for Indians is not available, it is impossible to pinpoint the exact beginning of their fertility decline; however, some child-woman ratios for the nineteenth century can be constructed for New York State Indians, who were enumerated in several state censuses. Published, aggregated data on age and sex allow for the construction of child-woman ratios: the ratio of children ages 0–4 to women of childbearing ages (ages 15–44) multiplied by 1,000. Child-woman ratios compare the number of young children to the number of potential mothers and are a standard measure for determining a population's overall fertility.[28] The child-woman ratios for New York State Indians were 725 in 1855, 675 in 1865, 693 in 1875, and 636 in 1930.[29] The fluctuations obscure when their fertility decline started, but the overall decline between 1855 to 1930 was very small. Evidence in chapter 3 will suggest that fertility levels in most Indian tribes had not yet started to decline in 1900.

Figure 1.2 compares Indian fertility with white and black fertility from 1910 to 1980. Data on age and sex were tabulated in U.S. census publications on Indians beginning in 1910. Figure 1.2 captures the tail end of the fertility decline among whites and blacks and suggests a new trend in differential fertility by race in the postwar period. Black fertility practically matched white fertility from 1910 to 1940 as both populations experienced fertility declines. Beginning during the baby boom, there was a growing divergence between blacks and whites; blacks began having considerably more children than whites (or whites began having fewer children than blacks).

Figure 1.2 shows that Indian fertility became synchronized with that of blacks and whites after World War II. In 1910 Indian fertility rates were not only higher than those of whites and blacks but were also changing at a different pace. Indian fertility may have then been in the early stages of decline but was interrupted by the postwar baby boom. During the baby boom, Indians making

FIGURE 1.2

Child-Woman Ratios, 1910–1980
(Ratio of Children 0–4 to Women 15–44)

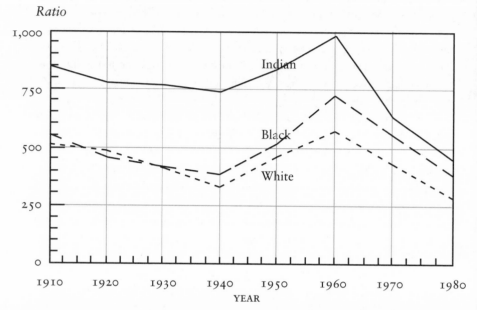

Sources: The child-woman ratios are based on age and sex distributions from the following U.S. Census Bureau publications (Washington, D.C.: GPO): *Historical Statistics of the United States: Colonial Times to 1970*, pt 1 (1975), 16–17; *1980 Census of Population; Characteristics of the Population, United States Summary*, vol. 1, pt. 1, ch. B (1983), 23, 31–33; *Fifteenth Census of the United States: 1930. The Indian Population of the United States and Alaska* (1937), 87; *Sixteenth Census of the United States: 1940. Population: Characteristics of the Nonwhite Population By Race* (1943), 7; *U.S. Census of Population: 1950. Nonwhite Population By Race*. Special Report, vol. 14, pt. 3, chap. B. (1953), 17; U.S. Bureau of the Census, *U.S. Census of Population: 1960. Nonwhite Population by Race* (1961), 2; *1970 Census of Population: American Indians* (1973), 2.

fertility decisions must have been influenced by the same economic and social incentives as other Americans, for even though they already had very high fertility, Indians shared in the baby boom at about the same pace as blacks and whites.[30] For the Indian population the post-baby-boom decline in fertility, usually referred to as "the baby bust," was precipitous. Some of the decline was no doubt due to the changing composition of the Indian population. In 1980, Indians living on reservations or in "historic (non-urban) areas of Oklahoma" did have a much higher child-woman ratio (661) compared to Indians nationwide (457).[31] People who changed their ethnic identity between the 1960 and 1980 censuses probably had lower fertility rates, bringing the overall rate down.

Both the population decline and subsequent population recovery had origins in some combination of changing mortality and fertility rates. Scholars studying the causes of population decline have emphasized the role played by mortality, particularly the catastrophic mortality brought on by the introduction of European epidemic diseases. Although less attention has been paid to how European contact might have affected fertility, Indian fertility levels were obviously unable to keep pace with this higher mortality until the Indian population started growing again after 1900. The overview of Indian demography provided in this chapter shows that changes in life expectancy and fertility fueled the population recovery in the twentieth century. It was not until the 1940s, however, that Indian life expectancy began to rise significantly. At the same time, Indian fertility rose to its greatest level during the postwar baby boom, a phenomenon affecting all Americans. Population growth after 1940 is thus easily explained. But then what explains why, in 1900, the Indian population reversed the centuries-long trend of decline and began its recovery?

THE POPULATION HISTORIES
OF FIVE TRIBES

Although unreliable population data, migration, and shifting tribal identities make constructing population histories difficult and complicated, these histories are requisite for understanding the process of decline and recovery. This chapter presents population histories for the Senecas, Cherokees, Red Lake Ojibways, Yakamas, and Navajos.

The major problem in figuring out the size of tribal populations at any given point in time stems from imprecise tribal boundaries. Definitions of "Cherokee" and "Seneca" can be just as variable as definitions of "Indian." Early estimates of tribal populations are especially suspect because tribal identities were often constructed in the process of colonization and because Euro-Americans applied inaccurate labels to Indian groups for their own convenience and out of ignorance.[1] Moreover, Indian communities were in constant flux, forming military alliances, intermarrying with other Indians, and adopting war captives, sometimes as slaves but more often as family members.

Later estimates benefit from a developing bureaucratic sophistication, but government agencies varied in how they aggregated Indian population totals, whether by reservation, linguistic group, official tribal enrollment, or unofficial tribal identity, either self-identified or identified as such by a census taker. Federal census reports listed Indians by tribal identity or by reservation, rarely both in a single census year. Although having perhaps the easiest of the population histories to construct, the Seneca Nation illustrates some of the problems. When New York State published the results of its nineteenth-century censuses, Indians were grouped by reservation. Since other Iroquois, mostly Cayuga, lived on the two Seneca Nation reservations, Cattaraugus and Allegany, the Seneca Nation population is not the simple sum of these two reservations. Federal census publications grouped the Senecas differently in different years—sometimes by reservation, sometimes as Iroquois, sometimes as clusters of counties that contained Indian reservations, and sometimes as Senecas, which then included the Tonawanda Band of Senecas and any Seneca Indians living off the reservation.

The most regular and detailed reports on tribal population size, those of the Office (later Bureau) of Indian Affairs (BIA), are also the most problematic. Although BIA agents gave population figures for Indians within their jurisdiction in their annual reports, and beginning in 1885 were instructed by the head office to maintain census lists of Indians enrolled at their agency, these records are notorious for overreporting and incompetent reporting. Overreporting was a natural by-product of a system in which agency resources were calculated on the basis of agency populations. BIA agencies were never supplied as well as they should have been, and perhaps even the most dedicated bureaucrats realized that they and the Indians they served could profit by inflated population figures. Or, at many reservations, especially the Navajo Reservation, agents simply had no idea how many Indians actually lived there and had no resources to conduct the censuses required by the commissioner of Indian Affairs.[2] Another complication is that, for most of its history, the BIA had no working definition of tribal membership. Even if BIA enrollment lists are trusted to be accurate, tribal membership was determined by agents, often arbitrarily, until the 1930s, when there was a concerted effort to establish criteria for who belonged to which tribe.

And yet, BIA population figures are often all we have. In some cases—for instance, for Red Lake Reservation—the figures appear consistent. In other cases, the figures are contradictory from year to year. Although the BIA annual reports for the New York Iroquois give detailed breakdowns by tribe and reservation, the figures fluctuate wildly with no explanation given for why the Seneca Nation in one year had 150 more people or 150 fewer people than the year before. Presumably the agent was reporting the number of people counted in the distribution of annuities (the treaty-stipulated annual payments made to the Senecas and other Iroquois), but why there was so much variability in who received annuities is unclear.

Although the 1900 census data sets analyzed in chapters 3 and 4 consist of Indians living within the geographic boundary of a reservation or otherwise designated Indian community, residence is not the best criterion for measuring Indian population size. The criteria used in the following population histories vary depending on what population data were available. Because Red Lake Ojibways are a small minority of all Ojibways in the United States, and once off the reservation are unidentifiable from other Ojibways in census records, I constructed their population history just for Indians living at Red Lake. Because of postwar urban migration, more people have ties to Red Lake than are captured in the recent figures on their population. For the Yakamas and Senecas, two parallel population histories are provided, one based on tribal identification and the other based on the number of Indians living on the Yakama and Seneca Nation Reservations. The Cherokee and Navajo population histories are of all Cherokees and Navajos living in the United States. For each population history, in cases of questionable or contradictory figures, I relied most on actual census counts. Although censuses often undercount populations, the BIA figures show even greater inconsistency.

THE SENECAS

The Senecas were the westernmost of the five Iroquois tribes or Five Nations, which became Six Nations upon admission of the Tuscaroras in the early 1700s. Scholars have estimated that at the time of European contact the Iroquois numbered about 20,000. They lived in politically allied villages with economies centered around agriculture and hunting. With the arrival of European traders, the Iroquois thrived economically but at a cost to their health. Beginning in the 1630s and continuing into the next century, European diseases, most often smallpox, swept through Iroquois country nearly every five to ten years. By the eighteenth century, the Iroquois had been reduced to a mere 11,000. Despite their small population, they had by then emerged as the most powerful Indian group in the region, partly due to their strategic position in the Northeast and the diplomatic and military capabilities of the Iroquois Confederacy. Incorporating other Indians and whites, by adopting captives taken in war, partly sustained their population.[3]

The Senecas were the largest of the Iroquois nations in population; exactly how much larger is, however, open to question since English colonists generally reported Iroquois population in terms of number of warriors (table 2.1; fig. 2.1). Colonial records from 1771 reported 4,000 for the Seneca population as a whole, but the American Revolution caused another population decline, the extent of which is also open to question. During the war the Senecas reluctantly sided with the British and fell victim to a U.S. military strategy of burning Indian crops and destroying villages. Thus the war left many Senecas dislocated, near starvation, and vulnerable to U.S. demands. When the war ended, the Senecas signed treaties with the United States in which they ceded land and agreed to live on several reservations in western New York. Many Senecas preferred living among

TABLE 2.1

Seneca Population, 1771–1980

Year	Population		Source
	All Senecas in U.S.	Indians Living on Seneca Nation Reservations	
1771	4,000		O'Callaghan, *Documentary History of New York* 4:1093
1789	1,137		Kirkland, "Census of Six Nations"
1819	2,128		Hough, *Census of the State of New York for 1855*, 517
1845	2,617		Schoolcraft, *Notes on the Iroquois*, 25
1855	2,557	2,003	Hough, *Census of the State of New York for 1855*, 500
1865	2,817	2,242	Hough, *Census of the State of New York for 1865*, 601, 603
1875	2,977	2,352	Hough, *Census of the State of New York for 1875*, 464
1890	2,967	2,560	Donaldson, *Extra Census Bulletin: The Six Nations of New York*, 6
1910	2,907		U.S. Census Bureau, *Indian Population* (1910), 20
1970	4,644		U.S. Census Bureau, *1970 Census of Population: American Indians*, 155
1980	7,220	2,764	U.S. Census Bureau, *American Indians, Eskimos, and Aleuts* (1980), 1; *Characteristics of American Indians by Tribes* (1980), 23

Note: (1) All Senecas in the U.S. includes those living on New York State reservations (Allegany, Cattaraugus, Tonawanda, and before 1848 Buffalo Creek), at Neosho Agency in Indian Territory beginning in 1845 (ranging from 125 in 1845 to 215 in 1910), those living on the Cornplanter Grant in Pennsylvania (numbering 51 in 1845 and 87 in 1890), and where available, as in the twentieth-century census figures, those not living on reservations. When exact figures were not given for Neosho or Cornplanter Senecas, I estimated their population size. (2) The Senecas at Allegany and Cattaraugus formed the Seneca Nation in 1848. For 1855, 1865, and 1875, I added an estimated 70 people to include the Cornplanter Grant, often considered part of Allegany. In the nineteenth century, there were about 200 non-Seneca Iroquois living at Allegany and Cattaraugus, mostly Cayugas, and they are included in the population figures for Indians living on the Seneca Nation reservations, though estimated in 1865 and 1875. (3) The U.S. Census reported a decline of 1,000 in the Iroquois population from 1910 to 1930 but credited this decline to a great number of New York State Indians listed without a tribal designation; see U.S. Census Bureau, *Indian Population* (1930), 42. (4) In 1980, 4,068 Indians listed "Iroquois" as their tribe, some of whom were probably Senecas but not recorded as Senecas; Snipp, 327.

FIGURE 2.1

Seneca Population, 1771–1980

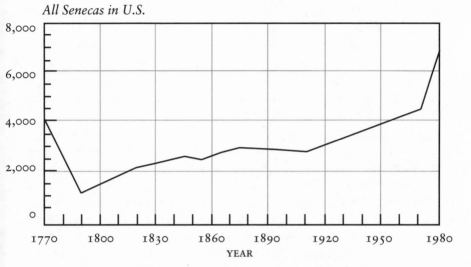

the British and stayed in Canada or moved there. The 1789 population figure of 1,137 comes from a census conducted by the missionary Samuel Kirkland, but given the increase in population apparent several decades later, it seems likely that Kirkland's census undercounted the Seneca population residing on the U.S. side of the international border.[4]

As the Senecas adjusted to life on a reservation, they also struggled to retain their lands. Federal and state government officials pursued fraudulent means to negotiate a treaty in the 1830s that would have required removal westward. Most Senecas resisted removal; however, several hundred Senecas and Cayugas eventually did settle permanently in Indian Territory. The Senecas remaining in New York, with the advocacy of the Quaker Church, protested the fraudulent removal treaty and won a compromise. They lost some of their land—a large reservation lying within the booming city of Buffalo—but retained part of three other reservations: Allegany, Cattaraugus, and Tonawanda. In response to their chiefs having assumed too much power in signing away their lands, the Senecas living at Cattaraugus and Allegany formed the Seneca Nation in 1848. This new government, based on a written constitution and laws, established elected officials and a court system to hear civil disputes. The Tonawanda Band of Senecas kept their traditional form of government.[5]

In the late nineteenth century the Senecas successfully resisted government efforts to allot their lands to individuals, and in the twentieth century they less successfully fought New York State's flooding of part of the Allegany Reservation for Kinzua Dam, built in the 1960s. Otherwise, the Seneca Nation government has retained the lands and governmental structure established in the nineteenth century.[6] The Senecas' population history reflects the increased stability of their political situation. After recovering from the crisis brought on by the American Revolution, the Seneca population grew from about 2,600 people in 1845 to 2,900 people by 1910. In the twentieth century, the Senecas experienced rapid population growth (fig. 2.1; table 2.1).

The threat of removal and, for a few Senecas, actual removal probably had some impact on population, but disease was also a factor in constraining their population growth in the nineteenth century. U.S. Indian agents in New York reported smallpox epidemics occurring at Allegany in 1862, at Tonawanda in 1866, and at both Cattaraugus and Allegany in 1889. Measles also struck; an especially dangerous epidemic was reported at all the Iroquois reservations except Tuscarora in 1873. In 1890 there were twelve reported deaths from measles at Cattaraugus. All these epidemics resulted in fatalities, though considerably fewer deaths than would have been caused by the same diseases in the seventeenth century. With about ten deaths per epidemic, most often of children, European diseases among the Iroquois in the late nineteenth century were declining in virulence.[7]

Of the six Iroquois tribes, the Mohawks had the fastest growing population in the nineteenth century. The Akwesasne, or St. Regis (Mohawk), reservation population nearly tripled in size between 1855 and 1890, while the combined population of Allegany and Cattaraugus had added only one-fourth of its 1855 population by 1890. And yet the Mohawks also seem to have had an especially stressful disease history, with frequent epidemics of cholera, typhus fever, smallpox, and measles.[8] Although the Mohawks and Senecas had different relations with Canadian Iroquois because Akwesasne straddles the international border, migration of Mohawks into the United States does not explain their population growth either. New York State censuses did report well over a hundred Mohawks with Canadian birthplaces compared to fewer than twenty Senecas, but it is likely that similar numbers of Mohawks with American birthplaces had moved to the Canadian side and were being reported in Canadian censuses.[9] Epidemic diseases and migration were factors in population growth but, in and of themselves, are insufficient explanations for different growth rates among tribes.

The causes of earlier population decline—warfare, removal, land loss, and especially disease—were in recession in the nineteenth century. However, even though the population reached some stability in the mid- to late- nineteenth century, it was not until the twentieth century that the Senecas experienced significant population growth. There must have been other factors that kept their population from truly recovering until the twentieth century.

THE CHEROKEES

When Europeans arrived in North America, the Cherokees had been living for at least several hundred years on lands now lying within the Carolinas, Tennessee, and Georgia. The earliest European accounts of the Cherokees come from sixteenth-century Spanish explorers of the Southeast. They noted that epidemic disease and depopulation had recently occurred in many of the villages they visited but did not remark upon the size of the Cherokee population. Because colonial documents reporting Cherokee population size date from the 1700s, we have only estimates for the earlier period. James Mooney estimated the Cherokee population in 1650 to have been 22,000; Peter Wood has recently suggested it was closer to 30,000 or 35,000.[10]

Historical documents from the early eighteenth century give figures for the Cherokee population ranging from 12,000 to 16,000, a sharp decline that suggests European contact had already taken its toll (table 2.2; fig. 2.2). As with the Iroquois, European trade linked the Cherokees to global markets and led to an influx of new material wealth but simultaneously increased the incidence of warfare and epidemic disease. A major crisis hit the Cherokees in 1738 when, according to the trader James Adair, smallpox "reduced the Cherokee population by half."[11] This was their worst recorded epidemic. By 1800 the Cherokees had suffered through at least three other known epidemics and had also fought in a series of wars against the Iroquois, Creek, English, French, and eventually Americans.[12]

During the American Revolution most Cherokees sided with the British and were later forced to sign treaties with the United States ceding land and establishing reservation boundaries. In the fifty years following the treaty agreements, federal government officials, the southern states, and squatters pushing the American frontier westward persistently tried to deprive the Cherokees of these lands. As they organized against these attempts, the Cherokees' government became increasingly centralized, while at the same time well-educated mixed-bloods led other Cherokees in a policy of cultural accommodation. Political leaders developed a constitution, written laws, and a court system modeled after the U.S. government. Many Cherokees became wealthy merchants, planters, and slave owners. Cherokee leaders encouraged Christian missions to settle and establish schools, and a newly invented Cherokee syllabary rapidly made literacy in the Cherokee language widespread.[13]

TABLE 2.2

Cherokee Population, 1721–1980
(All Cherokees in the U.S.)

Year	Population	Source
1721	12,000	Mooney, *Historical Sketch of the Cherokee*, 24
1735	16,500	Ibid.
1738	8,250	Adair, *History of the American Indians*, 232–34
1809	13,395	McLoughlin and Conser, "Cherokees in Transition," 681; Everett, *Texas Cherokees*, 10; Thornton, *The Cherokees*, 47–48
1818	16,044	Mooney, 97
1825	17,563	Mooney, 104; McLoughlin and Conser, 681
1835	21,542	Mooney, 119; McLoughlin and Conser, 681; Thornton, "Cherokee Population Losses," 295
1851	18,726	Wardell, *Political History*, 84
1867	15,566	Wardell, 216
1871	16,482	ARCIA (1871)
1880	17,908	Thornton, *The Cherokees*, 104–5; Wardell, 235
1890	25,015	U.S. Census Office, *Indians Taxed and Not Taxed*, 255, 501
1910	31,489	U.S. Census Bureau, *Indian Population* (1910), 15
1930	45,238	U.S. Census Bureau, *Indian Population* (1930), 59
1970	66,150	U.S. Census Bureau, *1970 Census of Population: American Indians*, 144
1980	232,080	U.S. Census Bureau, *Characteristics of American Indians by Tribes* (1980), 8

Note: (1) These figures are for "Cherokees by blood" and exclude intermarried whites, black slaves or freedmen, and other Indians. (2) Thornton's *The Cherokees* gives a detailed history of Cherokee population. The figures given here generally are the same figures and sources (e.g., Mooney) determined by Thornton to be the most accurate, with two exceptions. I have used Wardell's summary of the 1851 census instead of Thornton's (p. 82) figure of 16,231, for which Thornton's source was *The New American State Papers*, 12: 309. The 1851 census reported 16,593 Western Cherokees with an additional 2,133 to account for the Eastern Cherokees. Second, the 1880 Cherokee Nation census, as reprinted in two tables in Thornton (p. 105), reported two different figures for Western Cherokees, 15,150 and 15,307, with no explanation for the discrepancy. The Cherokee Nation later added 601 people to the 1880 census list. I have used the 15,307 figure, adding the missed 601 people and an estimated 2,000 Eastern Cherokees. (3) Western Cherokees are estimated at 1,000 in 1809, 3,500 in 1818, 4,000 in 1825, and 5,000 in 1835. After removal to the west, there were a recorded 2,000 Eastern Cherokees in 1867. The 1890 figure consists of 3,000 Eastern Cherokees and 22,015 in Indian Territory.

FIGURE 2.2

Cherokee Population, 1721–1980

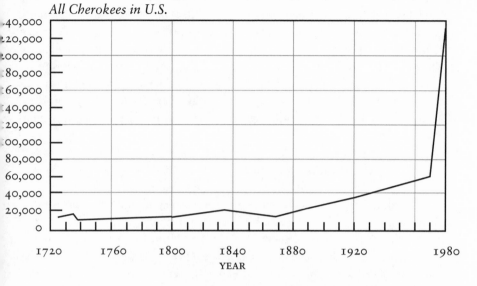

A census conducted in 1809 resulted in a total count of 13,395 people (table 2.2), but by then Cherokee dispersal and the incorporation of whites and blacks had begun to confound calculations of the total population. Some Cherokees migrated to Texas, eventually joining bands of Kickapoos and other Indians. Other Cherokees voluntarily emigrated west to Arkansas under removal plans sponsored by the federal government. In the 1820s to mid-1830s the majority of Cherokees lived in the Georgia and Tennessee area, while 3,000 to 5,000 Cherokees lived in Arkansas Territory.[14] A rising ethnic heterogeneity within the Cherokee Nation occurred at the same time. Intermarriage with whites, although common among white traders and Cherokee women in the 1700s, became even more commonplace in the nineteenth century. The Cherokee Nation also incorporated a black minority, almost all of them bought and held as slaves. William McLoughlin and Walter Conser's analysis of the 1835 census of the eastern Cherokees listed 16,542 Cherokees, only 77 percent of whom were full-bloods. Also listed were 201 intermarried whites and 1,592 black slaves.[15]

In the winter of 1838–39 the U.S. government forcibly removed the main body of Cherokees, still residing in the Southeast, to Indian Territory, to what is now the northeastern corner of Oklahoma. About a thousand or so Cherokees avoided removal by hiding out in the hills of North Carolina. The United States later recognized their descendants as the Eastern Band of Cherokees and established a small reservation for them in North Carolina. Most Cherokees, however, traveled the Trail of Tears to the new Cherokee Nation in the west, suffering disease, death, and hardship along the way. The standard estimate for the number of deaths is 4,000, which constituted one-fourth of those removed to Indian Territory in the late 1830s. Russell Thornton argued that the losses were much higher. The 4,000 figure refers to deaths during the trip, but the stress of removal, which led to malnutrition and increased vulnerability to diseases such as cholera and influenza, had long-term debilitating effects, including a probable reduction in fertility. Thornton suggested that total losses, not just deaths, numbered more than 10,000.[16]

After removal the Cherokee Nation was plagued by political turmoil caused largely by tensions between the old settlers, who had removed to the west earlier, and the new arrivals. Within a few years Cherokee leaders negotiated a reunited government, which seemed to be working until another crisis intervened: the Civil War. Violence between rival factions led to more economic hardship and political uncertainty. During the war the Cherokee population again dropped dramatically (table 2.2), though actual fighting had a minimal role in this decline. Harsh conditions in refugee camps—starvation, exposure to cold winters, and disease, including an 1863 smallpox epidemic—caused many deaths.[17]

In 1867 the U.S. government forced another treaty on the Cherokees as punishment for their having initially sided with the Confederacy. This treaty required that former black slaves, as well as Delaware and Shawnee Indians settled in the nation, be admitted to tribal rolls as Cherokee citizens. Thus, for most of the nineteenth century, the Cherokee Nation was pluralistic. Census rolls reflected these ethnic divisions by indicating whether individuals were "Cherokees by blood," intermarried whites, slaves (or "freedmen," as they were called after the war), Delawares and Shawnees, or other Indians who had married Cherokees and lived within the nation's borders.[18]

The Cherokees prospered economically until the end of the nineteenth century, when the United States, intent on Indian assimilation, abrogated the tribal government. The 1898 Curtis Act called for the dissolution of the Cherokee Nation, which in 1907, now broken up into individual allotments, became part of the newly formed state of Oklahoma. In the twentieth century two tribal organizations emerged—the Cherokee Nation of Oklahoma and the United Keetoowah Band of Cherokee Indians, also based in Oklahoma—but, unlike the Eastern Band of Cherokees, neither has a reservation.[19] After the Civil War and throughout the twentieth century the Cherokee population grew rapidly.

Figure 2.2 summarizes changes in the Cherokee population from the eighteenth century to 1980. If there were more figures available for the eighteenth century, the period from 1738 to 1809 would no doubt look more jagged, with frequent declines interrupting rapid population growth. Population probably increased between these periodic crises.[20] In the nineteenth century the Cherokee population grew rapidly, interrupted by two devastating events: removal to Indian Territory in the winter of 1838–39 and the Civil War. In figure 2.2, the effects of removal and the war merge as one steady decline because population figures are available only for 1835, 1851, and 1867. Although disease epidemics continued to occur within the Cherokee Nation throughout the nineteenth century, none seem to have had as definite an impact on population as removal and the war.[21] However, no matter the cause of the crisis, the Cherokees quickly recovered from population loss whenever it occurred.

In the twentieth century the Cherokee population continued to grow rapidly, now uninterrupted by epidemic disease, forced removal, or the political and economic instability brought on by war. The spectacular growth since 1970 is primarily due to the popularity of Cherokee ancestry among people reclaiming an Indian identity. Historically high rates of white and Cherokee intermarriage partly explain why so many people today talk about their "Cherokee grandmothers." But also the Cherokees have a well-known history and brand-name appeal (Cherokee Jeans and Cherokee Jeeps, for instance), which probably attract some people who know they have an Indian heritage but do not know for sure which tribe.

RED LAKE BAND OF OJIBWAYS

At the time of European contact the Ojibways (also known as Chippewas or Anishinabeg) lived among other Algonquian-speaking peoples in the Northeast. They were leading participants in the transatlantic beaver fur trade, and Ojibway society and culture changed in many ways as a result. The fur trade led to a fleeting economic prosperity and population growth, and the Ojibways began to exploit larger areas of land, migrating westward in search of more productive hunting territories. By the nineteenth century most Ojibways were living north and west of the Great Lakes—in Canada, Wisconsin, and Minnesota. As the Ojibways moved westward, warfare increased, especially with the Dakotas, upon whose lands they had encroached.[22]

The earliest historical accounts of Ojibways living at Red Lake, located several hundred miles west of Lake Superior in what is now northern Minnesota, are records of fur traders dating from the late 1790s and early 1800s. At that time the Red Lake Ojibways, probably consisting of several different bands, hunted furs for trade and, for their own consumption, relied mainly on fish, corn, wild

TABLE 2.3

Red Lake Ojibway Population, 1805–1980
(Indians Living at Red Lake)

Year	Population	Source
1805	700	Wheeler-Voegelin and Hickerson, *Chippewa Indians I*, 213–14
1823	500	Ibid.
1824	200	Ibid.
1832	290	Ibid.
1843	315	Ibid.
1847	400	Ibid.
1850	800	ARCIA (1850)
1866	1,183	ARCIA (1866)
1871	1,049	ARCIA (1871)
1880	1,128	ARCIA (1880)
1890	1,120	U.S. Census Office, *Report on Indians Taxed and Indians Not Taxed*, 336
1900	1,338	Red Lake Data Set (see appendix)
1910	1,357	1910 U.S. Census Manuscripts for Red Lake, National Archives Microfilm Collection T624
1950	3,004	U.S. Census Bureau, *Nonwhite Population by Race* (1950), 62
1960	2,908	U.S. Census Bureau, *Nonwhite Population by Race* (1960), 211
1970	2,741	U.S. Census Bureau, *1970 Census of Population: American Indians*, 143
1980	2,826	U.S. Census Bureau, *American Indians, Eskimos, and Aleuts* (1980), 155

rice, and maple sugar. The first estimates of the number of Indians living around Red Lake come from fur traders who reported that a smallpox epidemic had severely depopulated all Lake Superior Ojibways in 1780–83 and that as of 1800 the Indians at Red Lake had not yet recovered from this epidemic.[23]

Table 2.3 and figure 2.3A show an unstable population size at Red Lake for the early nineteenth century. This instability is explained not only by Ojibway migration and settlement patterns but also by the varying perceptions that traders and explorers held about which Ojibway bands lived in the area. Although the evidence suggests that the Red Lake population grew by several hundred people from 1800 to 1860, this growth may have been due to consolidation and the migration of more Ojibways to the Red Lake area and not to natural increase.

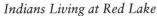

FIGURE 2.3A
Red Lake Ojibway Population, 1805–1980

Indians Living at Red Lake

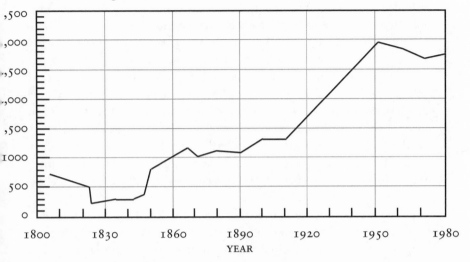

FIGURE 2.3B
Disease and Population at Red Lake, 1866–1907

Population (y-Logarithmic Scale)

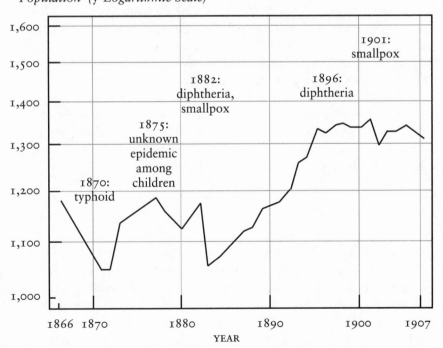

In the first half of the nineteenth century the depletion of beavers pushed the fur trade farther west, and white farmers began moving into Minnesota Territory. Although few white settlers sought Red Lake land because of its isolated location in the far north of Minnesota, the Red Lake Band sold large tracts to the United States in 1863, 1889, and 1904. Despite this loss of land, BIA agents reported favorable economic conditions at Red Lake for most of the nineteenth century. The second largest Indian reservation in Minnesota, Red Lake was perhaps the most fortunate in its dealings with the United States. In the mid- to late nineteenth century, the U.S. government removed most Minnesota Ojibways to a newly established reservation, White Earth. White Earth lands were later allotted to individuals, and much of the land was eventually lost through tax forfeiture and fraudulent sales. In contrast, the Red Lake Band remained at Red Lake, and their land was never allotted.[24]

In the latter half of the nineteenth century the Red Lake population grew slowly. Frequent, small-scale epidemics, often fatal for children not yet exposed to the disease, limited population growth. The regularity of the Red Lake agents' annual reports to the commissioner of Indian Affairs allows for closer study of the relationship between epidemic disease and changes in population. Figure 2.3B is an enlarged detail of the period from 1866 to 1907, with certain years marked to note the incidence of disease. The slow growth apparent in figure 2.3A, shown in more detail in figure 2.3B, was the result of epidemic disease periodically interrupting rapid growth. Between epidemics there was population growth, and by 1900 epidemics had become less severe.

The Red Lake Band adopted a written constitution in 1918 and went on to develop its own court system, industries, schools, and social programs.[25] They also experienced their most rapid growth in the twentieth century. The drop since 1950 (fig. 2.3A) reflects migration away from the reservation to urban areas. In the early 1970s the tribal enrollment officer for Red Lake reported that there were about six thousand enrolled tribal members, many of whom lived in the Twin Cities or in other off-reservation locations.[26]

YAKAMAS

The Confederated Tribes and Bands of the Yakama (formerly "Yakima") Indian Nation originated in an 1855 treaty with the United States designed to settle, on a single reservation, fourteen tribes and bands: the Yakamas, Klickitats, Wishrams, Washos, Wenatchees, Walla Wallas, and others. Before the treaty these groups shared a common culture and way of life. They lived on the Columbia Plateau and were mostly Sahaptin-speaking peoples. Their economy was based on sea-

TABLE 2.4

Yakama Population, 1805–1980

Year	Population		Source
	Yakamas in U.S.	Indians on Yakama Res.	
1805	3,500		Anastasio, "The Southern Plateau," 202
1849	1,500		ARCIA (1850)
1854	600		ARCIA (1854)
1862	667		ARCIA (1862)
1871		2,000	ARCIA (1871)
1886		1,290	ARCIA (1886)
1887		1,741	ARCIA (1887)
1888		1,765	ARCIA (1880)
1890	1,143	1,423	U.S. Census Office, *Indians Taxed and Indians Not Taxed*, 603, 613
1900		1,620	Yakama Data Set (see appendix)
1910	1,362		U.S. Census Bureau, *Indian Population* (1910), 21
1950		2,826	U.S. Census Bureau, *Nonwhite Population by Race* (1950), 3B-62
1960	3,966		U.S. Census Bureau, *Nonwhite Population by Race* (1960), 211
1970	3,856	2,509	U.S. Census Bureau, *1970 Census of Population: American Indians*, 143, 147
1980	6,506	4,948	U.S. Census Bureau, *Characteristics of American Indians by Tribes* (1980), 50; *American Indians, Eskimos, and Aleuts* (1980), 9

Note: (1) The ARCIA figures sometimes distinguished between Indians on the reservation and Indians at that agency but not necessarily on the reservation. Thus in 1871 there were a reported 3,500 Indians attached to the Yakama agency, in 1875 an estimated 4,100, and in 1886 an estimated 3,290. (2) The 1890 census reported 943 Yakamas on the reservation and an estimated 200 off-reservation.

sonal migrations to fish for salmon, dig roots such as camas, and pick berries in the mountains. They traded among each other, met often at social gatherings, and intermarried extensively.[27]

Lewis and Clark, who traveled across the Columbia Plateau in 1805, noted that smallpox had devastated the tribes in that area about thirty years before. Angelo Anastasio estimated that at the time of Lewis and Clark's trip there were 3,500 Yakamas and Kittitas, 2,600 Klickitats, 2,200 Wishrams and Washos, 1,600

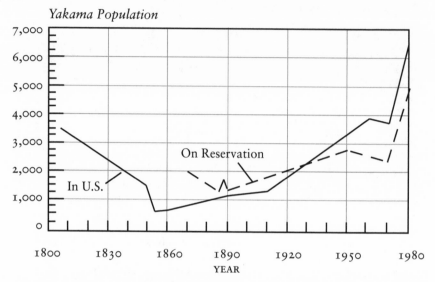

FIGURE 2.4

Yakama Population, 1805–1980
(All Yakamas in the U.S. and Indians
Living on the Yakama Reservation)

Walla Wallas, and 1,000 Wenatchees. A second smallpox epidemic struck the Columbia Plateau around 1800, another in the 1820s, and two more in 1843 and 1853. By the mid-nineteenth century the Yakama population reached its lowest point of about 600 people (table 2.4; fig. 2.4).[28]

The arrival of diseases coincided with increased trade between Indians and Euro-Americans. Later, the arrival of white settlers seeking Indian land led the Yakamas and others to sign, reluctantly, the 1855 treaty with U.S. emissaries. While the treaty was awaiting ratification, however, a series of misunderstandings and violent incidents erupted into full-scale war. The Yakima War as a historic event is perhaps most notable for its pan-Indianism, the partly successful attempt by Yakama chiefs to persuade and even "hire" other Indian groups to join them in fighting the United States. When the war ended a few years later most, but not all, of the Yakamas settled on the reservation laid out in the 1855 treaty.[29]

As different tribes and bands settled more permanently on the reservation, in-migration added to the population; however, there was also out-migration and a general confusion about who should be counted as part of the Yakama agency. In 1860, a hundred Lewis River Klickitats moved onto the reservation, and in 1879 the Paiutes were brought within the Yakama agency, but by 1883 many of them had left to settle at other reservations. Chief Moses's band of Columbia Indians was briefly included with the Yakama agency as part of the 1855 treaty, but they never resided there and eventually settled on the Colville Reservation.[30]

Calculating the Indian population for the Yakama agency is made more problematic by the alleged inflation of BIA figures. In 1881 James Wilbur, who had been the Yakama agent for about fifteen years, felt compelled to defend his annual population estimate, which he said "has been pronounced in a certain quarter as a monstrous exaggeration."[31] Excluding Moses's band, Wilbur claimed there were 3,400 Indians within the Yakama agency, consisting of 2,302 permanent reservation residents (mostly Yakamas and Klickitats), 472 Paiutes, 598 Indians who lived on the reservation only during the winters, 276 "Disaffected Indians" who lived off the reservation entirely, and 350 Palouse Indians who were not on the reservation yet but were to be removed there soon. The unclear boundaries of who belonged to the Yakama Confederated Tribes obscure whether migration, natural increase, or both were responsible for the rise in population apparent in the late nineteenth century. However, consolidation within the bounds of the reservation by the turn of the century is the most likely cause of the population increase since the 1890 federal census reported that the Yakamas were "decreasing, and the same cause may be cited here as elsewhere. Syphilis in the secondary forms, scrofula, and consumption prevail."[32]

In the twentieth century, as the Yakama population began a more definite recovery, the Yakama Reservation was also becoming more stable economically and politically. The reservation was allotted at the turn of the century, and as happened on most allotted reservations, non-Indians quickly acquired reservation land. However, the Yakama Nation resisted the sale of surplus lands and thus retained more tribally owned land than most other allotted reservations: of the original 10 million acres set aside for their use in the 1855 treaty, they managed to hold onto 1.3 million acres. In the 1930s the Yakamas chose not to organize their government following the guidelines set by the Indian Reorganization Act and instead developed a strong tribal government independently. In the more recent past the Yakama government has pursued irrigation projects, contested water and fishing rights, and tried to rebuild their tribal land base.[33] In the early 1970s they had a tribal enrollment of about six thousand members, two-thirds of whom lived on the reservation.[34]

Yakama population history reveals a pattern similar to those of the other tribes discussed previously (fig. 2.4). Initial contacts with Euro-Americans brought on severely depopulating bouts of epidemic disease. The Yakamas began recovering from these diseases in the late nineteenth century but did not experience rapid population growth until the twentieth century.

NAVAJOS

The Navajos are today the largest Indian tribe in the United States with an official tribal enrollment of about 200,000 members.[35] They also reside on the largest Indian reservation, most of which lies within Arizona and New Mexico on lands the Navajos occupied before European contact. At that time the Navajos were not an especially large tribe. A Spanish account from the early 1600s mentions a gathering of 30,000 *Apaches de Navajò*, but scholars consider this figure much too high and estimate instead a population well under 10,000.[36]

The Navajos described in early Spanish accounts were primarily agriculturalists, but the Spanish conquest of Mexico and the arrival of sheep and horses in the Americas gradually transformed their way of life. After the 1680 Pueblo Revolt, when Pueblos briefly succeeded in ridding their towns of Spaniards, many Pueblos fled and joined Navajo families, bringing their sheep and knowledge of weaving with them. Later, by raiding Indian towns and Spanish settlements, the Navajos began to amass large herds of sheep and horses. By the nineteenth century they had become one of the most powerful Indian tribes in the Southwest. Trade in food, animal hides, and especially slaves brought them into contact with Mexicans, Hopis, Pueblos, Paiutes, Utes, and Apaches.[37]

The effects of this rapidly changing economy on Navajo population are difficult to judge. The Navajos traded in slaves but were themselves also the victims of a large slave trade centered at Santa Fe. The acquisition of large herds of animals may have improved the health and security of the Navajo people, but surely it led to increased raiding and warfare. When the United States acquired Mexico's territorial claims to the Southwest, there was still a tendency to inflate the size of the Navajo population. Denis Johnston, in his detailed study of Navajo demographic history, estimated that on the eve of the Civil War the Navajos numbered fewer than 15,000, but he also admitted that Navajo population size before the twentieth century remains a mystery.[38]

The Navajos became the subjects of bureaucratic record keeping during the Civil War as the United States carried on a simultaneous campaign against the Navajos. The U.S. Army rounded up Navajo men, women, and children and in 1864 forcibly removed them to an arid, inhospitable patch of land called Bosque Redondo, near Fort Sumner, in New Mexico. The Navajos call this the Long Walk and consider it the worst period in their history. Death and disease were rampant. The water at Bosque Redondo was scarce and undrinkable. Crops failed, and there was insufficient grass for grazing animals. Finally, U.S. government officials, realizing that Bosque Redondo had only made the Navajos dependent on the U.S. government for their support, responded to Navajo appeals for the return of their old lands and in 1868 signed a treaty assigning them a reservation in Arizona Territory on lands they had previously occupied.[39]

TABLE 2.5

Navajo Population, 1867–1980

Year	Population	Source
1864–8	8,000	Johnston, *An Analysis of Sources of Information on the Population of the Navaho*, 132
1869	8,181	ARCIA (1870)
1872	9,114	ARCIA (1872)
1874	11,068	ARCIA (1874)
1879	15,000	ARCIA (1879)
1886	17,358	ARCIA (1886)
1890	17,204	U.S. Census Office, *Indians Taxed and Not Taxed*, 155
1910	22,455	U.S. Census Bureau, *Indian Population* (1910), 19
1930	39,064	U.S. Census Bureau, *Indian Population of the United States* (1930), 40
1970	96,743	U.S. Census Bureau, *1970 Census of Population: American Indians*, 146
1980	158,633	U.S. Census Bureau, *Characteristics of American Indians by Tribes* (1980), 28

Note: (1) The 1864–8 figure refers to Navajos at Bosque Redondo and excludes those held as slaves in Mexico and those who managed to escape captivity. Johnston (p. 133) summarizes the different estimates of how many Navajos were not at Bosque Redondo. The estimates range from 500 to over 2,000. (2) See Johnston, pp. 133–39, for more discussion of BIA and census figures for the period from 1869 to the 1960s. (3) The Census Bureau in *Indian Population of the United States* (1930), p. 40, acknowledged that there was probable undercount in both the 1910 and 1930 censuses, since the BIA reported 28,000 Navajos in 1910 and 42,000 Navajos in 1932.

The army's military campaign against the Navajos resulted in many deaths of Navajos deemed "hostile," those who resisted being taken prisoner. There was also high mortality on the Long Walk itself. As Navajos were ruthlessly herded toward Bosque Redondo, those unable to keep pace with the soldiers were killed along the way. The subsequent years spent at Bosque Redondo also saw considerably more deaths than births. Bimonthly statistical reports for Bosque Redondo for 1865 show a steady decline in the Navajo population from 8,510 in March to 8,477 in May, 7,173 in July, and 7,151 in August. The arrival of more Navajos by September raised their population to 7,318.[40] Throughout their captivity the population at Bosque Redondo remained at about 7,500 (table 2.5). Newly captured Navajos periodically brought to the reservation obscured the extent of mortality by making the recorded population size appear stable. There were at least several hundred Navajos who escaped Bosque Redondo altogether, but their lives were still disrupted, endangered, and preoccupied with the need to defend themselves.[41]

FIGURE 2.5

Navajo Population, 1867–1980

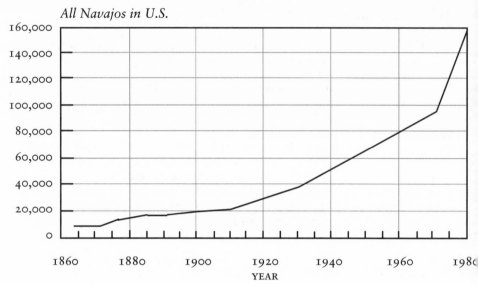

All Navajos in U.S.

After leaving Bosque Redondo in 1868, the Navajos prospered, primarily by raising sheep as well as goats, horses, and cattle. In 1869 the United States distributed 15,000 sheep and goats to 8,181 returning Navajos. By 1900 their livestock numbered in the hundreds of thousands. Anglo traders established trading posts on or near the reservation to deal in Navajo wool, blankets, and silverwork. Navajo population growth and their need for a large land base to support their growing herds resulted in periodic additions to the reservation. In the hundred years after the 1868 U.S.-Navajo treaty, the Navajo Reservation grew to more than twice its original size.[42]

Beginning in the 1920s, government policymakers, attempting to "rationalize" the Navajo economy, introduced a stock-reduction program and the concept of a business council to facilitate the use of Navajo land for mineral exploitation. Stock reduction, implemented in the 1930s, impoverished many Navajo families and was comparable to the Long Walk as a particularly painful moment in Navajo history. Stock reduction had no apparent effect on the human population of the Navajo Reservation, however, given the remarkable growth experienced in the twentieth century. The anger most Navajos felt about U.S. government interference in their stock raising did have a political impact and helped transform the business council of the 1920s into the powerful tribal government of today's Navajo Nation.[43]

Navajo demography has been more thoroughly investigated than that of any other tribe in the United States.[44] And yet, the reasons for their phenomenal growth in the nineteenth and twentieth centuries are unclear. Part of the mystery of Navajo population growth can be explained as improved record keeping; by the twentieth century increasingly more Navajos fell within the purview of bureaucracies producing statistical records. Most of the Navajo growth in population must, however, be the result of exceptionally low mortality and high fertility.

Research has shown that the Navajos had lower mortality than other Indian tribes in the nineteenth century, especially compared to their Hopi neighbors, who lived close together in small villages atop mesas. The Navajos, in contrast, lived at great distances from each other. The Navajo dependence on stock raising encouraged a dispersed residence pattern, which may have incidentally prevented the spread of epidemic disease. In the late nineteenth century the Hopis experienced several devastating smallpox epidemics, while the Navajos did not.[45] The worst recorded epidemic among the Navajos was the 1918–19 influenza epidemic, but even though nearly two thousand Navajos died from it, the long-term growth of the Navajo population seems to have been little affected (fig. 2.5).[46]

SUMMARY

Despite the problems entailed in constructing the population histories of these five tribes, there is sufficient evidence to show that Indian tribes recovered from population loss at different times and different paces. Still, tribes also experienced many of the same demographic events. All five of these tribes declined in population at some point in their histories. The major cause behind decline was the onslaught of newly introduced epidemic diseases of European origin. Except for the Navajos, all these tribes were diminished, sometimes by as much as half their population, by a smallpox epidemic occurring in the early stages of Indian–Euro-American contact: the Senecas in the seventeenth century, the Cherokees in the early eighteenth century, and the Red Lake Ojibways and Yakamas around the turn of the nineteenth century. An increase in Indian resistance to these diseases made the population recovery possible.

Abdel Omran's model of an "epidemiologic transition" provides one way of understanding changes in the disease environment for Indians at the turn of the century. He articulated a three-period transition. In the first stage, the "Age of Pestilence and Famine," epidemic disease is the major cause of death and leads to periodic mass mortality and sudden drops in the population. In the "Age of Receding Pandemics," infectious diseases decline in virulence, and sustained population growth begins. In the third, low-mortality period, the major causes of death are "Degenerative and Man-Made Diseases." Rapid population growth occurs even though there is a simultaneous decline in fertility.[47]

Indian morbidity and mortality patterns in 1900 had reached Omran's "Age of Receding Pandemics," and slow but sustained population growth occurred. Sudden bouts of epidemic disease among Indians were rare. Smallpox and measles had evolved into children's diseases, still a significant health threat but not life-threatening as earlier in the century. However, chronic, infectious diseases still posed an equally serious health problem. Tuberculosis emerged as the major cause of death among Indians and continued as such through the 1940s. Nonfatal but debilitating diseases such as trachoma and venereal disease added to Indian health problems in the early twentieth century. Today Indians are less likely than whites to die from degenerative diseases such as heart disease but are more likely to suffer from diabetes, alcohol-related diseases, and accidental death. Most literature on Indians and the epidemiologic transition places contemporary Indians at Omran's third stage.[48] Omran's theory accommodates the pattern of recovery shared by most Indian tribes: a period of slow growth in the early twentieth century followed by more rapid growth later in the century.

The emphasis on epidemic disease as the major cause of the population decline should not, however, mislead us into thinking that the conquest of these diseases alone explains the population recovery. Political crises arising from Euro-American expansion, especially removal, constituted the second major cause of decline: the Cherokee Trail of Tears in 1838–39 and the Navajo Long Walk in the 1860s. By 1900 Indians within the borders of the United States had become fully settled as "wards of the government" within the reservation system. Government-sponsored crises, such as removal, occurred less often, but government policies such as the boarding school system and poorly funded reservation health care programs meant that chronic mortality among Indians remained high.

Indian populations began growing again at the turn of the twentieth century in part because catastrophic mortality lessened. However, resistance to epidemic disease and shifts in government policy are insufficient explanations for the Indian population recovery that began in 1900. The Senecas were the first tribe to succumb to the violent effects of European diseases and therefore, one might think, should have been the first tribe to develop a resistance, and yet in the early stages of their population recovery they experienced only minimal population growth. And the two tribes that lived through removal, the Cherokees and Navajos, had the fastest growing populations.

Table 2.6 compares population increases for each tribe for a sixty- to seventy-year period ending in 1930. The erratic nineteenth-century population figures for the Yakamas make any calculation of their turn-of-the-century population increase suspect. Clifford Trafzer has suggested that many Indians living on the

TABLE 2.6

Population Increase for Each Tribe, 1860s–1930

Population	Number	Percent
Seneca (tribal identity)	669	24
1865: 2,817		
1930: 3,486*		
Cherokee (tribal identity)	29,672	191
1867: 15,566		
1930: 45,238		
Red Lake (residence)	997	84
1866: 1,183		
1930: 2,180*		
Yakama (tribal identity)	1,526	229
1862: 667		
1930: 2,193		
Yakama (residence)	344	17
1871: 2,000		
1930: 2,344		
Navajo	31,064	388
1868: 8,000		
1930: 39,064		

*Interpolated linearly using closest figures from tables 2.1–2.5.

Yakama Reservation eventually came to identify Yakama as their tribal affiliation, which would explain the apparently rapid increase in population calculated according to tribal identity.[49] The 17 percent increase based on residence is probably a more accurate indicator of Yakama population growth and fits the demographic characteristics of the Yakamas in 1900 (described in chapter 3). If residence is used as the criterion for measuring population increase, the Yakamas had the slowest rate of increase of these five tribes. The Navajos had the fastest growth, followed by the Cherokees. The Red Lake Ojibways had a slower rate of growth, but still their population grew more quickly than that of the Senecas. Other factors besides catastrophic mortality—such as chronic mortality and fertility—must have had a role in determining when, why, and at what pace Indian tribes began their recovery.

CHAPTER THREE

MORTALITY AND FERTILITY IN 1900

The different paces at which the Senecas, Cherokees, Red Lake Ojibways, Yakamas, and Navajos recovered from population loss originated in vary ing demographic rates. This chapter compares mortality and fertility for the five Indian groups in 1900 using data from U.S. census manuscripts. For added perspective I have included whites and blacks in the analysis, using data from the 1900 *U.S. Census Public Use Sample* (see appendix).

MORTALITY IN 1900

There are no reliable vital registration records for Indians for the late nineteenth or early twentieth centuries. At that time the BIA attempted to institutionalize vital-statistics registration on Indian reservations despite BIA agents' persistent claims that they lacked the cooperation of Indian communities and that all their statistics grossly underreported vital events. Researchers who have used these BIA censuses as a source for vital information have found a dramatic rise in Indian mortality during the 1910s and 1920s. However, this apparent increase in deaths may have been an increase in the reporting of deaths.[1]

An alternative measure of mortality is made possible by two questions asked of women in the 1900 federal census: "How many children have you had (excluding stillbirths)?" and "How many of these children are still alive?" Demographer William Brass devised a method for constructing life-expectancy estimates

TABLE 3.1

Mortality, 1900
(Based on Proportion of Children Dead for Women, 20–44)

	Proportion of Children Dead	Estimated Life Expectancy at Birth	Number of Women, 20–44
Seneca	.36	30	341
Cherokee	.26	41	399
Red Lake	.37	30	211
Yakama	.47	24	311
Navajo	.11	58	305
White	.17	50	1,538
Black	.26	41	977

Note: Using a different sample of Navajo data from the 1900 federal census, Johansson and Preston arrived at a life expectancy at birth for the Navajo of 50 years. Using one especially careful enumerator's list, they arrived at a figure of 36 years, which they considered more plausible.

using survival rates of children based on these two variables and model life tables. Table 3.1 compares life expectancy at birth for the five Indian groups and for whites and blacks applying Brass's method to 1900 federal census data.[2]

With this method the estimated life expectancy at birth for whites is fifty years, close to the standard figure of forty-eight years given for whites in 1900 based on vital-statistics registration data. For blacks, Brass's method gives an estimated life expectancy at birth of forty-one years, while the estimate based on vital registration data for "Negro and Other" is a much lower thirty-three years. In 1900 the U.S. government collected vital statistics from a limited registration area of several states and the District of Columbia. Regional differences in mortality may have led to more bias in the mortality estimates for nonwhites.[3] In addition, Brass's method depends on accurate responses to the two questions on children ever born and children surviving. Because women might be more likely to forget dead children than living children when reconstructing their childbearing histories, the proportion of children surviving at the time of the census could be overstated. Estimates of life expectancy based on the proportion of children dead should be considered optimistic; actual life expectancy for Indians was probably lower than the figures provided here.[4]

This analysis arrived at an exceptionally high life expectancy for the Navajos of fifty-eight years. Enumerators among these five Indian groups did not indicate any difficulty in eliciting accurate responses from Indian women about their childbearing histories. However, Navajo women gave nearly identical responses to the children-ever-born and children-surviving questions, and this number usually matched the number of children in the household. In an article comparing Hopi and Navajo demography using the 1900 census manuscript forms for the Hopi Reservation, Johansson and Preston derived a life-expectancy estimate of fifty years for the Navajos but concluded that this was too high. The data collected by one especially careful enumerator led to what they considered to be a more plausible thirty-six years. Johansson and Preston speculated that Navajo women underreported the number of children ever born because they were reluctant to mention the dead for fear of attracting ghosts.[5] The following discussion of fertility confirms that Navajo women indeed understated the number of children ever born.

Navajo life expectancy was probably not quite fifty-eight years but still must have been high, perhaps as high as Cherokee life expectancy, given the phenomenal increase in the Navajo population. At forty-one years, Cherokee life expectancy was not as high as that for whites but was equivalent to black life expectancy. Life expectancy among the Senecas and Red Lake Ojibways was considerably lower, an estimated thirty years. The children of Yakama women in all age groups from twenty to forty-four suffered higher mortality than any of the other populations, resulting in a life expectancy of twenty-four years.[6]

FERTILITY IN 1900

Tribes with the highest mortality did not make up those losses with high fertility. Table 3.2 compares total fertility rates in 1900 derived from a variety of measures. Total fertility rates are the number of children a woman would have had if her childbearing experience summarized the experience of all women in a designated age group, in this case either ages 15–44 or 20–49. The first two columns of table 3.2 give total fertility rates calculated from the number of children resident in the household with their mother. This measure, usually referred to as "mean number of own children," does not rely on women's responses to retrospective fertility questions. Own-children measures of fertility have their own biases, however, since some children and mothers will have died, will be living in separate households, or will be undercounted in the census. Since infants tend to be undercounted in censuses, I have added to the more standard measure of own-children ages 0–4 the second column of total fertility rates based on own-children ages 5–9. This measure is not necessarily more accurate since, of course, children ages 5–9 might also be more likely to live apart from their mothers than children ages 0–4. These own-children measures were adjusted for child mortality before being used as the basis for calculating total

TABLE 3.2

Total Fertility Rates, 1900

DERIVED FROM			
Mean Number of Own-Children 0–4 for Women 15–44	Mean Number of Own-Children 5–9 for Women 20–49	Mean Children Ever Born, Women 15–44	Mean Total Fertility Rate
Seneca	5.5	4.3	5.9	5.2
Cherokee	5.8	6.2	8.1	6.7
Red Lake	5.8	5.9	6.3	6.0
Yakama	4.5	4.0	5.9	4.6
Navajo	5.0	5.7	5.1	5.3
White	3.5	4.1	4.7	4.1
Black	3.9	5.0	5.3	4.7

Number of women ages	15–44	20–49
Seneca	410	395
Cherokee	622	491
Red Lake	271	245
Yakama	362	365
Navajo	424	358
White	2,015	1,759
Black	1,350	1,116

Note: Before being used to compute total fertility rates, the mean number of own-children figures were adjusted for mortality using life expectancy rates from Table 3.1 to reverse-survive children under five and ages 5–9 using Coale and Demeny's Model Life Table—West: Cherokees—table 10, Senecas and Red Lake—table 6, Yakamas—table 3, using the conservative estimate of 36 years for the Navajo—table 8, for whites—table 13, and for blacks—table 10. For a similar application of this method, see Mason, Weinstein, and Laslett, "The Decline of Fertility in Los Angeles, California, 1880–1900." To arrive at total fertility rates, I totaled the age-specific rates.

fertility rates. The third column is a total fertility rate based on children-ever-born (the number of children women told the census enumerator they had had).[7]

Using three different measures confirms the pattern of differential fertility among these five tribes, even though the total fertility rates vary depending on their derivation. Except for the Navajos, the children-ever-born total fertility rates are all systematically higher than the own-children rates, confirming that Navajo responses to the children-ever-born question did leave out some children and that own-children measures are a better indicator of Navajo fertility.

TABLE 3.3

Effective Fertility, 1900

	Mean Number of Own-Children × 1,000 (Unadjusted for Mortality)		Number of Women, Ages	
	Children 0–4 for Women 15–44	Children 5–9 for Women 20–49	15–44	20–49
Seneca	625	431	410	395
Cherokee	742	731	622	491
Red Lake	641	573	271	245
Yakama	458	341	362	365
Navajo	605	614	424	358
White	481	536	2,015	1,759
Black	497	581	1,350	1,116

To lessen some of the irregularities in these three measures, the fourth column of table 3.2 averages the three total fertility rates to arrive at a summary figure for each population. When all three total fertility rates are taken together, the Cherokees had the highest fertility, followed by the Red Lake Ojibways, Navajos, Senecas, and Yakamas. A Cherokee woman would have had close to seven children on average, while at the other extreme a typical Yakama woman had fewer than five children. All Indian groups had higher fertility than whites in 1900. Yakama and black fertility was essentially the same.

Table 3.3 gives the mean number of own-children ages 0–4 and 5–9 unadjusted for mortality, which is a good indicator of effective fertility, the number of children a woman might expect after taking the high mortality of early childhood into account. Tribes with the highest mortality show a big decline from the mean number of own-children 0–4 to own-children 5–9, reflecting that many children did indeed die before age 5. The Cherokees and Navajos had the highest effective fertility, as apparent in the second column of table 3.3. Although the Red Lake Ojibways had higher fertility than the Navajos, their effective fertility was lower because fewer Red Lake Ojibway children survived to adulthood. The two low-fertility groups, the Senecas and Yakamas, also had high mortality. They had fewer children to begin with, and then a large percentage of these children died before age 5. This was particularly the case among the Yakamas. In contrast, white and black women had more children in the 5–9 age group than in the 0–4 age group, a trend that probably has more to do with the fertility decline than with mortality.

The fertility decline is the subject of table 3.4, which assesses trends in fertility by comparing the number of children ever born for women at the end of

TABLE 3.4

Completed Fertility, 1900

	Mean Number of Children-Ever-Born to Women, Ages			Number of Women		
	55–70	45–54	35–44*	55–70	45–54	35–44
Seneca	5.6	5.0	4.9	89	89	130
Cherokee	5.2	6.1	6.2	55	100	94
Red Lake	6.0	4.8	4.9	57	74	80
Yakama	5.1	5.2	5.0	94	83	90
White	5.1	4.4	4.0	290	353	496
Black	6.9	6.4	4.8	147	180	147

*Not yet completed fertility.

their childbearing years, divided into three age groups (ages 55–70, 45–54, and 35–44) but excluding Navajo women since their children-ever-born responses were demonstrably questionable. Although women in the 35–44 age group had yet to finish their childbearing, I included them to show the minimum number of children ever born for this younger age cohort. Since these figures on completed fertility apply to women who bore most of their children a generation or two before 1900, a decline should be evident for those populations experiencing fertility decline. The fertility decline then occurring among whites and blacks is apparent in these figures. As other research has shown, black fertility had started declining later than white fertility but by 1900 was declining at a faster pace.[8] Indian fertility trends are not so easily discerned. Cherokee fertility appears to have been increasing. Seneca, Red Lake, and Yakama fertility was apparently stable but with fluctuations. None of the tribes could be said to have begun their fertility decline.

By modern standards, an average of five to seven children born per woman would be considered high fertility; however, five children is low for a nonindustrial, pre-demographic-transition society. Whites and blacks began their fertility declines from much higher starting places. Indian fertility in 1900 also conflicts with theoretical assumptions about fertility behavior in nonindustrial societies because the relationship between mortality and fertility was not a simple one in which women compensated for high mortality by having more children. If mortality compensation had been the primary factor in women's fertility decisions, Yakama women would have had the highest fertility. In all societies there are constraining factors that keep fertility from reaching the highest possible levels.

Most obviously, fertility depends on the frequency of sexual intercourse, which in turn is regulated by social norms of marriage and sexuality. Among the sexually active, there are other limits on fertility, some of which are deliberate, such as birth control, and others of which are factors beyond a woman's control, such as sterility caused by disease.

In Europe and Euro-America, marriage has, until recently, been a major determinant of fertility levels, and as some scholars have argued, perhaps even a deliberate strategy to control population growth.[9] Marriage also played an important role in shaping Indian fertility patterns, even though, of course, marriage for Indians in 1900 was conceptually different from marriage in Euro-American societies. For Euro-Americans marriage was a definite state of the life course, marked by a ceremony and a legal document. Although some Indians in 1900 were married by missionaries or granted licenses by federal or tribal government officials, most Indian marriages were more flexible arrangements that allowed for easy separation and remarriage. Some Indian societies marked marriage with a ceremony. In Yakama society, for instance, marriage involved a ritual exchange of gifts between families, usually a year or two after the couple had lived together and proven their compatibility. In many Indian societies, however, couples simply chose to live together or came to live together in family-arranged marriages.[10]

Without ceremonial beginning and ending points, marital status was an ambiguous category, sometimes a matter of individual opinion. In *Son of Old Man Hat,* an autobiography describing events in the late nineteenth century, a Navajo man tells how he spent the night with a woman at her hogan and afterwards said to her, "You've got a husband, and I'm afraid of him." She responded, "I want you to marry me, and now we have, we're married. So you're mine." Later, when the young man's uncle warns the couple that her husband will kill them both, she says, "I haven't got a husband. A man comes once every three or four months or once in summer and in winter. I don't call that a husband. So I want to let that fellow go, and I'd like to stay with him." Unfortunately, the autobiography ends at that point and all we know is that Son of Old Man Hat's new wife "stayed with us that night and never did go back." Imagine a census taker making his or her rounds in the midst of this shift in marriage partners. Everyone had a different opinion about who was married to whom.[11]

Despite the differing cultural understandings of what a marriage was, Indian and non-Indian responses to the census question about marital status were probably referring to the same thing in practice: cohabitation or, at the very least, extended sexual relations. Few whites may have cohabited without marriage, but if they were cohabiting, they would no doubt have told the census taker they were married.

TABLE 3.5

Percentage of Women, Ages 40–49, Who Never Married, 1900

	Percentage Never Married	Number of Women 40–49
Seneca	1.7	117
Cherokee	2.7	113
Red Lake	2.5	81
Yakama	1.0	98
Navajo	0.0	77
White	11.3	425
Black	5.7	211

Tables 3.5 and 3.6 compare marriage patterns in 1900 and show that Indian women from each of these five tribes were much more likely to marry than either white or black women. Table 3.5 gives the percentage of women ages 40–49 who were listed as never married. Table 3.6 summarizes women's marital status by treating women under age 50 as a synthetic cohort and determining an average number of years spent in each marital state.[12] For example, a Cherokee woman whose experience summarized the experience of all Cherokee women under 50 years old would have spent 22.3 years single, 23.1 years married, and altogether 4.6 years in what could be called a disrupted marital state: a year of

TABLE 3.6

Number of Years Spent in Each Marital Status
(Based on a Synthetic Cohort of Women, Ages 0–49)

		Married				
	Single	Spouse Present	Spouse Absent	Divorced	Widowed	N
Seneca	21.0	23.3	1.8	0.4	3.5	810
Cherokee	22.3	23.1	1.0	0.2	3.4	1,459
Red Lake	22.4	20.3	0.8	2.0	4.5	530
Yakama	19.4	23.5	0.5	2.7	4.0	656
Navajo	18.5	23.2	3.0	1.4	3.9	858
White	25.9	20.8	1.1	0.1	2.0	3,623
Black	24.3	19.0	2.0	0.2	4.6	2,495

TABLE 3.7

Marital Fertility, 1900
(Mean Own-Children, Ages 0–4, for Currently Married Women,
Ages 15–44, Spouse Present in the Household)

	Mean Own-Children, 0–4, for Currently Married Women, 15–44 (× 1,000)	Total Fertility Rate	N
Seneca	1,121	6.6	273
Cherokee	1,257	7.4	467
Red Lake	1,222	7.3	146
Yakama	1,040	6.0	236
Navajo	1,024	6.0	250
White	928	5.5	1,068
Black	1,034	6.1	641

Note: (1) Married Indian women population includes non-Indian women with Indian spouses. (2) These figures have been adjusted for mortality using the same method as described for table 3.2.

having a spouse absent, two or three months divorced, and about three and a half years widowed.

As tables 3.5 and 3.6 show, marriage was nearly universal among Indian women. In stark contrast to the more than 10 percent of white women who had never married, in all tribes less than 3 percent of women in their forties had never married (table 3.5). Indian women also spent more years in a married state, largely due to their marrying at younger ages (table 3.6). Except for the Red Lake Ojibways, an average Indian woman living to 50 years would have spent about 23 years married with her spouse present. Ever-married Indian women, as well as black women, however, were also more likely than whites to be living without a spouse, mostly because of high mortality and the consequently high rates of widowhood. The larger percentage of married women with a spouse absent among the Navajos probably includes some women in polygamous marriages who were living in their own hogans. For Indian women in 1900, early marriage and nearly universal marriage prevailed, conditions that should have led to very high fertility in the absence of other fertility control measures.

Table 3.7, which gives figures on marital fertility using the own-children 0–4 measure to capture the most recent fertility, shows that marital fertility followed the same general pattern as fertility for all women, as presented in table 3.2. The Cherokees had the highest fertility, with a marital total fertility rate of 7.4 children. The Red Lake Ojibways also had high fertility. The Senecas, Yakamas, and

Navajos had higher marital fertility than whites and about the same as blacks. Within marriage, white and black fertility levels were closer to Indian fertility levels, confirming that marriage patterns were an important source of the differences in Indian and non-Indian fertility. For whites in particular, overall fertility was substantially lower than marital fertility because white women married late and a large percentage never married at all.

And yet, among the Navajos, marriage reduced the potential for high fertility. Navajo women had the youngest age at marriage, and all Navajo women married, but they had low marital fertility rates compared to the other Indian tribes. The extent of polygamy among the Navajos explains their relatively low marital fertility. Research into the effects of polygamy on fertility has found that women in polygamous marriages have fewer children than women in monogamous marriages, which in turn can be explained by less frequent sexual intercourse.[13] The 1900 census listed 7.6 percent of Navajo married men living with more than one wife, but the extent of polygamy was undoubtedly much greater since Navajo men usually did not live with all their wives at the same time. Most wives had separate households, sometimes miles apart.[14]

Polygamy would not have affected fertility levels for the other tribes. The Senecas had never sanctioned polygamy. The Cherokee Nation gradually eliminated polygamy in the mid-nineteenth century by passing a series of laws against it. Although for most of the nineteenth century polygamy had been a part of Yakama and Ojibway society, usually among chiefs or other men of authority, by 1900 it was rare. The U.S. government, through its Courts of Indian Offenses, outlawed polygamy in the 1880s, which limited its practice. However, polygamy was still common among the Navajos at the turn of the century since the Navajo Reservation was considered too large and bureaucratically unmanageable for enforcement of the government's assimilation programs. Thus despite marriage patterns that were otherwise favorable for high fertility, Navajo fertility levels within marriage may have been relatively low because many of these marriages were polygamous.[15]

Because Indian marriage patterns would have supported very high fertility, there must have been other factors, both voluntary and involuntary, that determined fertility levels. Louis Henry, in his classic survey of what he called "natural-fertility" populations, estimated that women in noncontracepting societies would have an average completed family size of eight to twelve children. Since Henry's formulation of the natural fertility concept, demographic research has provided enough evidence to suggest that every society has some knowledge of birth control: there is no such thing as a "natural-fertility" population.[16]

Indian societies had birth control methods, most of which were turned to after conception, although women also tried using charms and medicines for contraception. The most common form of limiting births available to Indian women was abortion, achieved with the use of plant abortifacients or pressure applied to the woman's abdomen. Cherokee women may at one time have practiced infanticide. The Cherokee Council in 1826 passed a law against any woman or women who committed "infanticide during her or their state of pregnancy"; however, the wording of this law suggests that the council intended to make abortion illegal. By the end of the century, the Cherokee courts had charged an occasional woman with "infanticide" and "abortion," and thus the practice of it must have continued after passage of the law. The Senecas also, in a different way, began prohibiting abortion when, in the early 1800s, the Seneca prophet Handsome Lake advised mothers not to help their daughters have abortions.[17]

Indian women thus had access to birth control, but the reasons and circumstances under which they used birth control are less clear. Eighteenth- and nineteenth-century accounts of the Senecas refer to "the reluctance of their women to bear children, prompting them to employ means to prevent an increase of maternal responsibilities," and to Seneca women having "become tired of bearing children to be slain in war."[18] On the other hand, Seneca folklore tells of how children are like knots on a string, and each woman has within her a determined number of children waiting to be born. In the 1830s one Seneca woman conversing about death with a missionary told him how she had once died but then had to come back because she had not yet borne all her children.[19] If they considered childbearing to be predestined, Seneca women probably sought not to limit the overall size of their families but to delay childbearing if circumstances called for it.

This certainly seems to have been the case with abortions among Navajo women held in captivity at Bosque Redondo in the 1860s. The army doctor stationed nearby remarked that the Navajo population was surely decreasing. He cited syphilis as one cause but stressed above all that "what does and will decrease the number of the tribe and finally wipe them out of existence is the extensive system of abortion carried on by the young women. You may remark how seldom it is a young woman has a child; in fact, none of the women, except they are thirty or forty, ever think of having one, if they can help it, so that two or three children are considered a large family."[20] This doctor did not consider the possibility that the scarcity of water and food made women wary of bringing children into the world under such harsh conditions. In general, Indian women may not have used birth control to aim at an ideal family size, instead turning to it when having another child would have been a burden.

Henry proposed that demographers could judge whether women were practicing deliberate family limitation by checking for when they stopped having children. Other historical demographers have since established stopping child-

FIGURE 3.1

Marital Fertility by Age, 1900
(Married Women, 15–44)

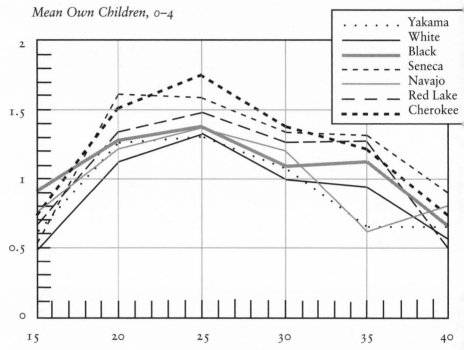

Mean Own Children, 0–4

	Yakama
	White
	Black
	Seneca
	Navajo
	Red Lake
	Cherokee

bearing as the main behavioral clue to discerning whether societies had adopted deliberate fertility control practices: once women have had a certain number of children, they decide to stop having children. However, research on the age pattern of childbearing in nonindustrial populations puts this assumption into question by having demonstrated that in societies in which women start childbearing at a young age, they also stop at a young age. The relationship between age at starting childbearing and stopping childbearing suggests that there might be other factors at work in determining when women end their childbearing.[21]

Figure 3.1 compares the age pattern of childbearing among these populations in 1900 using the mean number of own-children 0–4 for married women in five-year age groups, adjusted for mortality. The sharp dip apparent for Navajo and Yakama women in the 35–39 age group is probably a result of the extreme age heaping in these two populations (see appendix); the 40–44 age group includes many women in their thirties whose ages were recorded as 40 years. Otherwise,

TABLE 3.8

Starting and Stopping Childbearing, 1900

	Estimated Mean Age At		Differ-ence in Years	Number of Women	
	Starting	Stopping		15–49 (All)	40–49 (Mothers)
Seneca	20.7	33.2	12.5	453	58
Cherokee	22.0	37.1	15.1	650	84
Red Lake	22.4	37.8	15.4	301	47
Yakama	19.4	32.6	13.2	406	47
Navajo	20.2	34.6	14.4	421	49
White	24.2	34.5	10.3	2,161	265
Black	25.0	36.0	11.0	1,397	102

Note: (1) Starting is based on a synthetic cohort of women 15–49 using a method similar to singulate mean age at marriage. (2) Stopping is the age of the mother subtracted by the age of her youngest child still in the household.

the pattern of childbearing by age is similar for all groups, especially for women ages 20–39. Women in high-fertility populations had high fertility throughout their childbearing years, and vice versa. There was, however, more variability in when women started and stopped their childbearing.

To explore this further, table 3.8 provides estimates of when women in each population started and stopped childbearing. Estimated figures for starting childbearing were arrived at using a method similar to that for singulate mean age at marriage and are based on a synthetic cohort of women ages 15–49. To estimate the age at stopping childbearing, I limited the analysis to currently married women ages 40–49 and subtracted the age of their youngest child still present in the household.[22] These estimates should be considered approximate; however, they are consistent with the results shown in figure 3.1. Since Indian women married earlier than white or black women, it is not surprising that they also started their childbearing earlier. As in figure 3.1, table 3.8 shows that Seneca, Yakama, and Navajo women both started and ended their childbearing earlier than the other groups. Cherokee and Red Lake Ojibway women, even though they married later, had the longest span of active childbearing, estimated at about 15 years. Those tribes with a late age at stopping childbearing did have higher fertility, but it does not necessarily follow that Seneca, Yakama, and Navajo women were *choosing* to stop having children at a young age.

TABLE 3.9

Childlessness, 1900
(Percentage of Currently Married Women, Ages 30–50,
with No Children Ever Born)

	Percentage Childless	N
Seneca	13.6	213
Cherokee	4.9	247
Red Lake	10.5	114
Yakama	12.7	166
Navajo	9.6*	178
White	9.4	779
Black	10.8	351

Note: (1) Married Indian women population includes non-Indian women with Indian spouses. (2) *Since children ever born for the Navajos is understated, this figure is probably too high.

An alternative explanation for a young age at stopping childbearing is involuntary sterility and ill health. This is supported by comparing childlessness in these five tribes. At the turn of the century—whether Indian, black, or white—it would have been rare for a married woman to choose not to have any children at all. Table 3.9 compares childlessness in 1900 by giving the percentage of currently married women ages 30–50 who responded "0" to the question "How many children have you had?" Indians were not more prone to childlessness than whites and blacks, for the Cherokees had a remarkably low percentage of women without children. However, the Senecas and Yakamas had the highest percentages of childless women. Indeed, the three Indian groups with the highest mortality levels—Senecas, Yakamas, and Red Lake Ojibways—also had the highest percentages of childless women.

Another important component of overall fertility levels is child-spacing. Demographic research has demonstrated that women in nonindustrial societies space their children further apart than women in industrial societies. Some demographers have argued that child-spacing is a form of deliberate family limitation, since prolonged breast-feeding can reduce a woman's fecundity and delay the birth of the next child. There is more evidence, however, to suggest that child-spacing is a by-product of other intentions. In nonindustrial societies child-spacing seems to have been used as a way to maximize the survival chances of children already born. The health of a population could also determine particular patterns of child-spacing, for miscarriages and stillbirths would prolong the period

TABLE 3.10

Child-spacing for Women, Ages 15–44, 1900

Percentage of Women with at Least One Child Who Had Another Child Within Three Years	N
Seneca	46.8	47
Cherokee	70.3	91
Red Lake	48.1	27
Yakama	50.0	30
Navajo	65.8	117
White	62.7	406
Black	61.2	147

Note: This is limited to women whose children, based on the children-ever-born variable, were all still in the household and still surviving.

of time between births. It is unlikely that women anywhere have used child-spacing as a deliberate method aimed to limit the total number of children.[23]

Table 3.10 compares child-spacing in 1900 by showing the percentages of women with one or more children who had another child within three years.[24] Only about half of the Seneca, Ojibway, and Yakama women had had another child within three years, while among the other groups 60 to 70 percent of the women had already had another child. Again, since these three Indian groups also had the highest mortality, probably health conditions that could affect women's ability to conceive or could result in more miscarriages and stillbirths explain the differences in child-spacing. In addition, spacing their children far apart may have been some women's response to high mortality by encouraging them to invest as much as they could in each individual child.

Certain diseases likely to promote sterility were endemic in Indian communities at the turn of the century.[25] Venereal disease and genital tuberculosis can lead to temporary and permanent sterility for both men and women as well as higher rates of miscarriages and stillbirths.[26] Indian agency doctors often wrote that venereal diseases were widespread, but they had trouble diagnosing genital illnesses. All tribes in the Pacific Northwest, including the Yakamas, were reported as suffering from high rates of venereal disease, and agency officials believed it was the chief reason for the decline in the Northwest Indian population in the late nineteenth century.[27] Venereal diseases were also a problem among the Navajos, though mostly confined to areas near military outposts where U.S.

soldiers interacted with Navajo women.[28] Venereal diseases were a major health problem, but traditional Navajo and Yakama healing practices, which involved lengthy stays in sweat lodges, might have helped to limit the spread of diseases such as syphilis.[29] Prolonged exposure to heat is now thought to have some curing effect on venereal diseases. A heat box similar to sweat lodges was used as a cure for venereal disease in Europe in the 1920s and 1930s.[30]

While venereal diseases undoubtedly caused some involuntary low fertility, tuberculosis was the main culprit. Studies of tuberculosis among Indians conducted in 1907–8 and 1921 noted that Indians fell victim to tuberculosis more than whites and blacks. The earlier report, collected by the physical anthropologist Ales Hrdlicka, gave a tuberculosis death rate of 1.7/1,000 for whites and 4.0/1,000 for blacks. In contrast, most Indian tribes listed in Hrdlicka's study had death rates from tuberculosis in the 20–30/1,000 range. In 1912 the BIA reported 10.4 deaths per 1,000 for all American Indians, with 136 cases of tuberculosis per 1,000. So many Indians at the turn of the century were infected with tuberculosis that it must have lowered fertility levels.[31]

Hrdlicka reported that Indians in northern regions were most susceptible to tuberculosis, which would explain the higher mortality among the Yakamas, Senecas, and Red Lake Ojibways, but the effects of tuberculosis on fertility are less clear-cut. The Red Lake Ojibways had 23 deaths per 1,000 from tuberculosis according to the Red Lake Agency doctor's response to Hrdlicka's survey. Unfortunately, Hrdlicka did not have any statistics on the Yakamas and Senecas. Other accounts of Seneca health conditions confirm that by 1890 tuberculosis had become the major cause of death among the Senecas and that the incidence of tuberculosis was increasing at Allegany and Cattaraugus Reservations in the early twentieth century. The only Indians Hrdlicka reported as having a rate comparable to whites were the Navajos, for whom he gave a figure of 1.7 deaths per 1,000. Although Hrdlicka lacked specific figures for the Oklahoma Cherokees, the later study of tuberculosis among Indians reported that the Five Civilized Tribes were less troubled by the disease than most Indian groups.[32] Tuberculosis may have lowered fertility among the Yakamas and Senecas, but Red Lake fertility was relatively high despite the problem of tuberculosis. Tuberculosis alone does not explain the differences in fertility between tribes.

CONCLUSION

Indian populations had higher mortality and higher fertility than either whites or blacks in 1900. Marriage patterns explain why Indian fertility was higher. Indian women married young, and most Indian women married at some time in their lives. Within marriage, Indian women had only slightly higher fertility than white and black women. Even though Seneca and Yakama women ended their childbearing early, they married and started childbearing at a young age, making the span of years spent childbearing longer than that for whites or blacks. If, as some have argued, marital norms serve a larger demographic function by controlling population growth, these five Indian communities could be considered pronatalist. Indian women's marriage patterns should have led to very high fertility.

However, there were constraints on Indian fertility, which varied by tribe. The Yakamas and Senecas ended their childbearing at a young age, had high rates of childlessness, and spaced their children far apart. Despite their young age at marriage, these factors were sufficient in keeping their overall fertility the lowest of these five tribes. The Cherokees and Red Lake Ojibways had a later age at marriage but had the longest span of childbearing years and the highest overall fertility.

Chronic diseases, such as tuberculosis, could have been a major cause of these demographic differentials since, except for the Red Lake Ojibways, high-mortality tribes had low fertility and low-mortality tribes had high fertility. The Red Lake Ojibways, although they shared with the Senecas a low life expectancy at birth of thirty years, had fertility as high as that for the Cherokees. Demography is in itself insufficient in explaining the varying patterns. Cultural factors, such as polygamy among the Navajos, also played a role in determining these differences.

Although all five of these Indian groups had higher mortality and higher fertility than whites and blacks, there were also differences between the groups that influenced each population's recovery. These differences are consistent with the population histories presented in chapter 2. The Cherokees had the mortality and fertility rates most favorable for population growth. Navajo population growth was due mostly to their mortality rates, while fertility played a more important role in the less rapid population increase occurring among the Red Lake Ojibways. The Yakama and Seneca populations grew the slowest, not surprising given their fertility and mortality rates in 1900.

CHAPTER FOUR

THE ECONOMIC AND CULTURAL CONTEXT
FOR POPULATION GROWTH

U sing demographic theories as a starting point, this chapter assesses whether economic or cultural differences can shed further light on the varied demographic experiences of the Senecas, Cherokees, Red Lake Ojibways, Yakamas, and Navajos. Classic demographic-transition theory proposes that "modernization" (urbanization, democratization of education, increases in the standard of living, medical advances) caused the long-term declines in mortality and fertility known as the demographic transition. Modernization lowered mortality, and once parents realized that more of their children would live to adulthood, they had fewer children.[1] The idea of "modernization" has fallen into disrepute, but many of its components survive in more recent demographic theories, most of which point to either economics or culture as the cause of fertility differentials and trends.

Economic theorists argue that children are the product of a cost-benefit equation. Sometimes culture is accounted for with a variable labeled "tastes." In their simplest manifestation, economic theories of fertility suggest that children result from affordability; however, empirical research has yet to show that more wealth leads to more children in any society.[2] Determining whether economic well-being had any effect on Indian demography is hindered by the lack of a standard measure for Indian wealth or income in 1900. Indian economies were at that time in a transitional state. It was becoming harder to pursue traditional subsistence activities, and few new sources of livelihood had emerged to take their place. To survive, Indians adopted a multitude of economic strategies. All five of these tribes had access to some cash income from seasonal wage labor and, depending on the region, from selling products such as cotton, corn, maple sugar, the occasional animal hide, berries, roots and tree bark (sold to pharmacists), beadwork, blankets, baskets, and silver jewelry. There was also cash income from leased land and government annuities. Cash income was an indeterminable portion of total livelihood. The subsistence portion of native economies varied by region and tribe as well. For example, the Navajos raised sheep, grew corn, and collected piñon nuts, while the Red Lake Ojibways fished, hunted, trapped, grew corn, and gathered wild rice, maple sugar, and berries.

The 1900 census question about occupation highlights some of the difficulties in comparing economic conditions across tribes. Among the Cherokees and Senecas, nearly every man was listed as a farmer or farm laborer, a vague occupation applying both to big farming operations and small-scale subsistence farming. Except for a few silverworkers, all Navajo men were "sheepraisers," all Navajo women were "blanketweavers," and all Navajo adolescents were "sheepherders." Nearly all the Yakamas, including children, were listed as "hop pickers," since they gathered at hop picking camps in the summer to pick hops for wages. Among the Red Lake Ojibways, listed occupations included farmers, hunters, trappers, fisherwomen, and snake root diggers. In contrast, ten years later the U.S. census listed all Red Lake Ojibways' occupations as "Ration Indians" because they had just sold land to the U.S. government, and each individual received annuities.

The Great Lakes fur trade, the Oklahoma oil boom, lumbering, mining, and of course land sales brought fleeting economic prosperity, but these periodic economic booms amid rising, chronic poverty say little about how Indian families might have weighed childbearing decisions against their economic resources and expectations. Some tribes may have had more productive, stable economies. Perhaps the Cherokees and Navajos had lower mortality because they were wealthier, especially in their access to high-protein foods such as cow's and goat's milk. It is unlikely, however, that the Red Lake Ojibways, who had fertility levels comparable to the Cherokees, were having more children because they were wealthier than the other tribes and could afford them.

Even the more fine-tuned economic theories, such as Richard Easterlin's frontier thesis of fertility, provide little insight into Indian demography. In American history, frontier areas at an early stage of settlement and economic development experienced an increase in fertility levels. Easterlin explained this phenomenon with a formula combining the factors of land availability and the need for farm labor. The availability of farm land affected ideal family size because parents wanted to provide children with inherited land when they died. And the labor demands of farming made children's labor and large families a necessity. Once an area became settled, land became scarce, labor demands lessened, and fewer families depended on farming for a living; consequently, families became smaller.[3]

TABLE 4.1

Regional and Indian Fertility for All Women, Ages 15–44, in 1900

| | Total Fertility Rates | | N | |
	Indian	U.S./Region*	Indian	Region
Seneca	5.2	3.2	410	2,797
Cherokee	6.7	3.9	622	1,921
Red Lake	6.0	3.7	271	2,005
Yakama	4.6	2.6	362	780
Navajo	5.3	2.8	424	696

*Regional figures were based on analysis of the full 1900 U.S. public use sample for these regions:
  Cherokee Region: Indian Territory, Oklahoma, Kansas, Missouri, Arkansas;
  Seneca Region: rural New York State, Ohio, Pennsylvania (rural=places with fewer than 25,000 people);
  Red Lake Region: Minnesota, Wisconsin, Iowa, South Dakota, North Dakota;
  Yakama Region: Washington State, Oregon, Idaho, Montana, California;
  Navajo Region: Arizona, New Mexico, Colorado, Utah, California.

To test the possibility that regional development was a factor in Indian fertility levels, table 4.1 compares these five tribes to their surrounding regions. The total fertility rates for Indians are repeated from table 3.2, and equivalent figures for five regions within the United States were calculated using regional extracts from the entire 1900 *U.S. Census Public Use Sample.*

As Table 4.1 makes apparent, tribes with high fertility did live in regions with high fertility; however, Indians still had higher fertility than others in their region, which Easterlin's theory cannot explain. Indians were on the other side of the frontier. High Indian fertility in 1900 could not have been an expression of parental optimism about bequeathing land to children or a reflection of their need for farm labor. It was the dwindling Indian land base that made land available for frontier development. The government policy to allot reservation land to individual Indians at the turn of the century created a frontier situation in which Indians were expected to adopt the Euro-American values of private property and yeoman farming. Once implemented, however, the allotment policy hastened the loss of Indian land to non-Indian ownership.[4] Moreover, allotment apparently had no direct effect on demography. At opposite extremes in terms of their demographic patterns, the Cherokee and Yakama Nations were both in the process of being allotted in 1900. Also demographically very different, Red Lake, the Seneca Nation, and the Navajo Reservation were never allotted.

Cultural theories about fertility prove equally unsatisfactory. Theorists who point to culture as the cause of demographic change or difference argue for the diffusion of knowledge or custom. The most influential cultural theorist is John Caldwell, who argued that fertility declined as the spread of Western ideas, or "Westernization," as he calls it, reversed "wealth flows" within the family. In non-Western societies, parents benefit from children's labor, but with Westernization, parents begin investing in children. The biggest investment is education since once children are in school, they become consumers and are no longer producers within the family economy. This shift in cultural attitudes makes children more expensive, and large families become less desirable. Although Caldwell's theory is about a transition in cultural values, individual fertility decisions are still framed as part of a cost-benefit equation.[5]

The degree of "Westernization" among these five tribes can be compared with variables from the 1900 census on the ability to speak English and read (any language). Unfortunately, the 1900 census only asked whether the individual could speak English, and so we cannot know how many Navajos spoke Spanish and how many Ojibways spoke French. Table 4.2 gives the percentage who could speak English and read for the five Indian groups, as well as for whites and blacks.

In 1900 the majority of Senecas and Cherokees could speak English and read, compared to less than half of the Red Lake Ojibways and Yakamas. Among the Navajos, only a few people spoke English, and they were all in the youngest age group. In contrast, the Senecas and Cherokees had long histories of exposure to the English language, evident in how so many people in the oldest age groups could speak it. By the end of the nineteenth century the Senecas seem to have overtaken the Cherokees in their knowledge of the English language, with almost all Senecas able to speak English. The growing literacy gap between the Senecas and Cherokees might have been due to many older Cherokees being literate in the Cherokee syllabary, the writing system developed by Sequoyah in the 1820s.[6]

Figures on school attendance, provided in table 4.3, confirm that the Cherokees and Senecas were the most familiar with Euro-American culture. Large percentages of Cherokee and Seneca children attended schools. Seneca children went to school partly because New York State had a mandatory education law that extended to Indians living on reservations. Cherokee school attendance, though not nearly as high as that for the Senecas, reflects a long-standing Cherokee advocacy of school education. Before the 1898 Curtis Act called for dissolution of the Cherokee government, the Cherokee Nation had sponsored its own school system.[7]

The relatively low Seneca fertility in 1900, close to that of whites, could have been due to the Senecas adopting Western attitudes toward childbearing. However, Seneca fertility and marriage patterns, as presented in chapter 3, were

TABLE 4.2

Percentages of Indians, Whites, and Blacks
Who Can Speak English and Read (Any Language), 1900

	Percentage That Can Speak English	Percentage That Can Read	N
Seneca—ages			
10–24	98.0	85.0	439
25–49	96.5	73.7	659
50+	84.4	42.9	340
ALL AGES 10+	**94.1**	**69.9**	
Cherokee—ages			
10–24	84.6	78.9	1,064
25–49	82.7	77.6	680
50+	70.3	58.8	221
ALL AGES 10+	**82.3**	**76.2**	
Red Lake—ages			
10–24	44.3	38.7	341
25–49	14.5	8.9	372
50+	4.1	1.4	218
ALL AGES 10+	**23.0**	**18.0**	
Yakama—ages			
10–24	63.8	45.3	373
25–49	45.0	26.6	474
50+	20.7	4.6	261
ALL AGES 10+	**45.6**	**27.7**	
Navajo—ages			
10–24	2.1	1.1	567
25–49	0.8	0.2	502
50+	0.0	0.0	244
ALL AGES 10+	**1.2**	**0.5**	
White—ages			
10–24	98.0	95.2	2,562
25–49	96.9	94.4	2,890
50+	95.4	93.1	1,136
ALL AGES 10+	**97.1**	**94.5**	
Black—ages			
10–24	99.3	68.0	1,938
25–49	98.9	57.9	1,489
50+	99.1	23.9	576
ALL AGES 10+	**99.1**	**58.0**	

TABLE 4.3

School Attendance, 1900
(Percentage of Children, Ages 6–15, Who Attended School in Previous Year)

	Percent Attended	N
Seneca	71.5	354
Cherokee	48.5	932
Red Lake	29.6	334
Yakama	14.0	228
Navajo	0.6	532
White	62.4	1,923
Black	26.9	1,418

much more like those of other Indians than those of whites. Moreover, the other tribe most committed to sending their children to school, the Cherokees, had high fertility.

There may be economic and cultural explanations for the fertility differentials among Indians in 1900, but Indian demographic variability only serves to illuminate the inadequacy of existing theoretical models. Indians at the turn of the century could be considered premodern, nonindustrial, and non-Western. Indians had higher fertility than Euro-Americans, and their fertility was not at that time undergoing any decline. Indian fertility patterns appear alike when compared to those for whites and blacks, but Indian fertility also showed great differences from tribe to tribe. What explains these differences? Apparently not any of the reigning demographic theories.

There are hidden assumptions in demographic theories that make them awkward tools for understanding the Indian population recovery. Most obviously, as with all theorizing, demographic theories attempt to isolate a single cause for a complex process. They are doomed to fail. However, one side-effect of this simplification is that theorists encapsulate societies into two types: premodern and modern, nonindustrial and industrial, or non-Western and Western. "Pre" and "non" are clues that the world of demographic theory operates within a Eurocentric frame. These categories replicate the dichotomy of primitive and civilized discredited by other disciplines. Primitive versus civilized reduces cultural difference to a progressive time line, making European and Euro-American demographic experience the standard against which "non-Western" demographic experience is compared. "Non-Western" peoples are on the verge of becoming

TABLE 4.4

Percentage of Currently Married Indians
(Spouse Present)
Who Were Married to Whites in 1900

	Percent	N
Seneca	2.4	738
Cherokee	40.0	846
Red Lake	1.8	446
Yakama	2.0	742
Navajo	0.1	669

like Europeans.[8] Undeniably, Western culture has spread to other peoples around the globe, but that does not mean that "non-Western peoples" were, or are, all alike. Labeling American Indians premodern, pre-Western, or preindustrial does an injustice to the distinctiveness of their cultures and histories.

There is no single explanation for the variations in Indian fertility and mortality in 1900, but my research suggests that there were three economic and cultural differences among these five tribes that affected demographic experience: intermarriage, attitudes toward the accumulation of wealth, and household structure.

INTERMARRIAGE

Cherokee intermarriage with whites helped their population recover from population loss early and quickly. Of the five tribes, the Cherokees had the highest rates of intermarriage, most often with whites, since only a few Cherokees had black spouses. Table 4.4, which gives the percentage of married Indians who were married to whites for each of the five groups, shows the great extent to which Cherokees had intermarried by 1900. The number of Cherokees intermarried with whites was even increasing; table 4.4 includes all married people, regardless of age, but when married Cherokees were broken down into age groups, the percentage of Indians intermarried with whites was 51 percent for 15–29 year olds, 38 percent for 30–44 year olds, and 29 percent for 45–70 year olds.

Rates of intermarriage for the Red Lake Ojibways, Yakamas, and Navajos were low in 1900 partly because of lack of opportunity. Few whites had as yet settled in those regions. The Navajos, in particular, had so little contact with non-Indians that they were not likely to marry one. In contrast, the difference in rates of intermarriage between the Senecas and Cherokees marks a social difference between these two tribes.

Both groups had long histories of close contact with whites, beginning in the seventeenth and eighteenth centuries when white traders married Indian women, and when white captives taken in war were incorporated into Indian families.[9] By the mid-nineteenth century, however, the Senecas had established rules for citizenship that restricted the adoption or incorporation of non-Senecas. In framing a new government based on a constitution and written laws, the Seneca Nation preserved matrilineal descent as a system for determining tribal membership. If a Seneca woman married a white man, the children were Seneca; if a Seneca man married a white woman, the children were not afforded privileges in the Seneca Nation. They were, in a sense, tribeless Indians with no rights to reservation residence.[10] Not only would this policy have limited the number of racially mixed children eligible for tribal membership, but it also might have influenced Seneca men's marital decisions.

In contrast, the Cherokees disavowed their matrilineal past when they formed a constitutional government in 1827. It only took one Cherokee parent, of either sex, to produce Cherokee children. The Cherokees also allowed more non-Cherokees into the nation by granting them qualified citizenship status. The Cherokee government regulated intermarriage by passing a series of laws that permitted intermarried whites to settle in the nation for the duration of the marriage. Cherokee intermarriage laws became more restrictive in the late nineteenth century, but at the same time intermarriage increased as pressure to allot Cherokee land to individuals intensified. Because the Cherokee Nation was in the early stages of the allotment process in 1900, these census figures on Cherokee intermarriage probably include some people with dubious claims to Cherokee citizenship. Distributions of Indian land or trust money always attracted claimants, some completely fraudulent and others with stronger, albeit still tenuous, ties. Marriage records maintained by the Cherokee government, however, confirm the frequency of Cherokee intermarriage with whites in the latter half of the nineteenth century.[11] The Cherokee Nation's sanctioning of intermarriages with whites made the children of such mixed marriages fully accepted citizens of the Cherokee Nation, a social policy that undoubtedly enhanced Cherokee population growth.

Cherokee intermarriage with whites also affected population growth by raising fertility and lowering mortality. Table 4.5 compares fertility and mortality for three types of Cherokee couples: couples with at least one spouse listed as "full-blood," couples listed as "mixed-blood," and couples with one white spouse and one Indian spouse. There were too few cases to make reliable mortality

TABLE 4.5

Mortality and Fertility by Type of Marriage for Currently Married
(Spouse Present) Cherokees (Women, Ages 15–44) in 1900

Type of Marriage	Proportion of Children Dead	Mean Own-Children Ages 0–4 (× 1000)	N
Full-blood (one spouse or both)	.29	1,033	72
Mixed-blood (both spouses)	.24	1,085	97
White-Indian (one spouse white)	.18	1,129	223

adjustments, and so the figures on mean own-children under five were not adjusted upward to account for the children under age five who had already died.

Table 4.5 shows that children with one white parent and one Indian parent had the lowest mortality. Children with parents of mixed Indian-white ancestry had somewhat higher mortality but still lower mortality than children with at least one full-blood parent. The figures on fertility show a similar pattern with the highest fertility occurring among white-Indian couples; however, since these figures are close together and unadjusted for child mortality, fertility levels for these three groups were probably about the same. Within Cherokee society, there may not have been great differences in fertility levels, but overall Cherokee fertility may have been so high because they had for generations been intermarrying with whites. In other historical contexts, intermarriage between Indians and whites increased fertility. Research on the fur trade has shown that Indian women married to white men had high fertility as did Métis or "mixed-bloods," the offspring of white-Indian marriages. The 1910 U.S. census reported that full-blood Indians had considerably lower fertility than mixed-bloods. And, analysis of 1900 census data for the White Earth Ojibway Reservation and the Creek Nation in Oklahoma found the same pattern.[12]

There are several possible explanations for why intermarriage had this effect of boosting Cherokee demographic rates. Demographer Moni Nag provided one reason in his article on "How Modernization Can Also Increase Fertility."[13] Nag argued that "natural fertility" appears low in "premodern" societies because disease, lactation's effects on fecundity, and other factors constrained fertility; once such factors were removed by "modernization," fertility rose before it declined. Although the term "modernization" is problematic, it is reasonable to assume that Indians who married whites adopted some Euro-American child-bearing attitudes and practices. Abortion was perhaps no longer acceptable, and children may have been breast-fed for shorter periods of time, reducing the possibility of lactation limiting a woman's fecundity. Or, in a variation on Easterlin's and Caldwell's theories, Cherokees who married whites lived on the Indian-white frontier and may have had economic outlooks and needs that encouraged large families.

However, because Cherokee intermarriage lowered mortality, it was probably most significant for improving Indian health. Child-survival chances may have been greater for children of mixed couples because they had a higher standard of living, more access to medical care, and more resistance to disease. Ales Hrdlicka's study of tuberculosis conducted in the early twentieth century determined that contact with whites had spread the disease among Indians, but he noted that full-bloods tended to suffer from it at higher rates than Indians of mixed descent.[14]

Intermarriage helps explain Cherokee population growth, but it is not the only reason for differential demographic rates among these five tribes. The rapid population growth of the Navajos was not a by-product of intermarriage. Intermarriage may have helped the Cherokees resist disease, but the dispersed residence pattern of the Navajos and their lack of contact with whites limited their exposure to disease. If tuberculosis was the major constraint on Indian fertility at the turn of the century, then it would make sense that the two tribes with the lowest rates of tuberculosis would have the fastest growing populations.

ATTITUDES TOWARD THE ACCUMULATION OF WEALTH

The Navajos and Cherokees had another attribute in common in 1900 that exposes more of the hidden assumptions within demographic theory. Easterlin's idea of land availability is grounded in Western practices of property inheritance, and his prioritizing of labor demands presumes a farming economy. Both Easterlin and Caldwell treated land ownership and the labor of children as mechanisms for the larger, unstated goal of accumulating wealth for the family or for family patriarchs. They assume that people are motivated by a desire to accumulate wealth, as though this were a characteristic innate in humans and not part of a system of cultural values. The desire to accumulate wealth, an aspect of European culture, is thus made to appear universal. If families make fertility decisions for economic reasons, it is important to ask first about how their economy worked and what the cultural beliefs about wealth were.

Among these five tribes, only the Senecas and Cherokees had primarily agricultural economies in the early stages of European contact. These gradually became integrated with the surrounding regional farming economy in the nineteenth century. The Cherokees, however, had much higher fertility and lower mortality than the Senecas. The Red Lake Ojibways and Yakamas also had similar economies. At the time of European contact, they lived by seasonally migrating to fish, hunt, and gather roots and berries. In the early nineteenth century they became involved in the fur trade and by 1900 had a mixed economy of traditional subsistence activities and seasonal wage labor. And yet, the Red Lake Ojibways had very high fertility compared to the Yakamas. The Navajo economy, based on stock raising, was in a class by itself.

The type of economy seems to have had no bearing on Indian demography, but differing values about the accumulation of wealth might have. In the years before the Cherokees and Yakamas faced allotment of land to individuals, these five Indian nations shared the same basic concept of landholding on their reservations. The land was owned in common, but individuals or families could accumulate usufruct rights to communally owned land and thereby acquire wealth. Although all five tribes had landholding customs that allowed individuals to accumulate wealth, only among the Cherokees and Navajos did people do so to any great extent.

Few Yakamas and Red Lake Ojibways valued the accumulation of wealth, especially in land, since in 1900 they were still trying to maintain seasonal migrations of fishing, hunting, and collecting berries and roots despite set reservation boundaries. Their occupations, as listed on the 1900 census, show that most Ojibways and Yakamas were pursuing traditional gathering activities, though they now also sold some of what they gathered. Accumulating property would have burdened their ability to subsist off the land because they would have had to carry their property around with them or live on land lacking the desired variety of resources.

The Senecas, who had been agricultural people for as long as can be remembered, did not seem to value individual landholding either. Although it was possible to accumulate part of the communal land base by inheritance, purchase, or application to the Seneca Nation Council, few Senecas sought to accumulate large pieces of land. Most lacked the capital to develop a successful farm business, and those who had the capital were wary of investing it in land since they had lived first under the threat of removal and by the late nineteenth century were facing the threat of allotment. An 1888 New York State investigation into Indian affairs revealed the cultural distance between Senecas and whites, despite the Senecas' apparent assimilation of Euro-American language, clothing, and housing styles. Whites eager to open up the reservations accused Seneca men of being lazy since, as one white man living near the Allegany Reservation made the perhaps exaggerated claim, only one-twentieth of the reservation was under cultivation. One Seneca leader explained that most of the Seneca men worked very hard, "but they like to hire out; don't want to work for themselves."[15] Almost every Seneca family had some land cultivated, but most of this was for subsistence. A large portion of Seneca lands were leased to white farmers, who then employed Senecas as farm laborers.

In contrast, the antebellum Cherokee Nation saw the emergence of an elite class who accumulated wealth in land, slaves, and business enterprises such as ferries, toll roads, and stores. In late-nineteenth-century Indian Territory, individual Cherokees could acquire large tracts of common land with a permit from the tribal government allowing them to contract white sharecroppers to improve it. When the sharecropper's contract ended, the Cherokee holding the permit acquired the now improved land. Chief Charles Thompson, a full-blood Cherokee, spoke out against this practice in 1876: "I see in various portions of our country that there is greed and avariciousness manifested by some of our citizens to hold whole sections of land to the exclusion of other citizens, which I deem contrary to the constitution and should not be permitted."[16] Eventually allotment of Cherokee land made the struggle over property ownership a moot issue, but throughout the previous century, the pursuit of wealth by individual Cherokees had been a contested issue within Cherokee society.

Similarly, in the late nineteenth century Navajos valued the accumulation of wealth but also distrusted the wealthy. Because property was in sheep, which were mobile, and in silver jewelry, which was fairly compact, the Navajo economy was well suited to property acquisition. Land was also important insofar as usufruct rights to grazing determined the size of one's herd. Nevertheless, acquisitive tendencies among the Navajo were balanced by a strong ethic of sharing, especially among relatives, and anyone who seemed to acquire wealth at the expense of others could be accused of being "stingy" or, worse, of being a witch.[17] Still, Navajo culture in the late nineteenth century sanctioned the accumulation of wealth.

Profit maximizing even seemed to be associated with fertility. In the Navajo autobiography *Son of Old Man Hat*, the connection between accumulating wealth in sheep and the desire for more children is made explicit. A Navajo man pleading for the release of another Navajo wrongly held by U.S. troops argued, "A little while ago I said that we're all thinking about a long life and about getting something to eat all the time. We all want to raise more stock. We all want to raise more children. It's the same with Giving Out Anger. He's thinking as we're thinking now. He wants to live long. He wants to enjoy life. He wants to get more children, more stuff, more stocks, more of everything."[18]

The two tribes with the fastest-growing populations, the Cherokees and Navajos, shared reputations for valuing wealth and had built economies that allowed for its accumulation. They also had the highest effective fertility (fertility taking into account the high mortality years of early childhood). However, Red

Lake Ojibway fertility was also high, which neither rates of intermarriage nor the valuing of wealth can explain.

HOUSEHOLD STRUCTURE

Demographic theorists have resolutely misread the relationship between household structure and fertility. Following in others' footsteps, Caldwell predicated his "wealth flows" transition on a patriarchal, extended-family household turning into a child-centered, nuclear-family household. In general, demographic theorists have claimed that extended families and high fertility prevail in nonindustrial societies, the argument being that, in the economic context of a large kin group, extended relatives could help support the children or benefit from children's labor without having to bear any of the costs.[19] Contrary to theory, however, empirical research has found that women living in nuclear-family households have higher fertility than women in extended-family households. One common explanation is that the presence of extended relatives, particularly parents, limits the frequency of sexual intercourse.[20]

In 1900 the Senecas, Cherokees, Red Lake Ojibways, Yakamas, and Navajos structured their households in different ways, which may have had an impact on fertility. The tribes with the highest fertility, the Cherokees and Red Lake Ojibways, also had predominantly nuclear-family households. Table 4.6 compares household structures by giving the percentage of individuals who lived in nuclear-family households, in extended-family households, or as individuals living without relatives (as boarders, servants, or solitary individuals). Nuclear-family households consist of the head and any spouse or children, including stepchildren and adopted children. Extended-family households are defined as having at least one relative to the head who is not wife or child: mothers and fathers, in-laws, grandchildren and grandparents, nephews and nieces, aunts and uncles, brothers and sisters, and cousins.

As Table 4.6 shows, Indians were more likely than whites or blacks to live in extended-family households in 1900, with the Yakamas having the most complex households. As one government employee complained in 1892, "In visiting [the Yakamas] I frequently find two or more families in one house, sometimes living as one family; in other cases each family providing for itself. For this and other reasons it is difficult to tell the exact number belonging to each family."[21] Yakama household structure may have been determined by both economic necessity and cultural preferences.

The Senecas and Navajos also had more individuals living in extended-family households according to the 1900 census. The Senecas' history of extended-

TABLE 4.6

Household Composition, 1900

	Total Fertility Rate	Percentage of Individuals Living			
		In a Nuclear Family Hshold	In an Extended Family Hshold	Without Relatives	N
Seneca	5.2	53.6	39.4	6.9	1,982
Cherokee	6.7	66.9	29.5	3.5	3,092
Red Lake	6.0	66.3	31.5	2.2	1,338
Yakama	4.6	37.7	59.1	3.1	1,608
Navajo	5.3	59.4	39.2	1.4	1,921
White	3.5	71.0	19.7	9.3	8,828
Black	3.9	62.1	25.8	12.1	5,662

Note: Total fertility rates are reprinted from table 3.2.

family longhouses is well known. Although many scholars have accepted Anthony Wallace's argument (in *The Death and Rebirth of the Seneca*) that the prophet Handsome Lake encouraged the Senecas to adopt a nuclear-family social organization, it seems more likely that the longhouse religion helped maintain traditions, including living with relatives. In 1900 the Senecas were no longer living in multifamily longhouses, but there still seems to have been a cultural preference for complex households.[22] Navajo household structure evident from the 1900 census manuscript schedules reveals considerable enumerator variability, suggesting that each enumerator had a different idea of what constituted a household. The essential economic unit among the Navajo has been a matter of debate, with some scholars arguing for the centrality of the nuclear-family household, and others for the extended, matrilineal family or work group (which Clyde Kluckhohn and Dorothea Leighton called the "outfit").[23] Some enumerators seem to have used the nuclear-family hogan as the household; others may have taken several hogans together to be the household.

Some of the differences in household structure were due to married couples living with parents. Table 4.7 compares the percentages of married people living with their own or a spouse's parents. Although the Ojibways and Cherokees had similar percentages of individuals living in extended-family households, they had different patterns of family formation. As did whites, young married Chero-

TABLE 4.7

Percentage of Currently Married (Spouse Present) Individuals
Who Live with Parents or Spouse's Parents, 1900

	Percentage of		
	15–29 *year-olds*	*30–44* *year-olds*	N
Seneca	38.5	14.0	274
Cherokee	10.5	5.7	469
Red Lake	22.4	15.2	146
Yakama	33.3	25.0	238
Navajo	22.6	12.0	250
White	6.1	8.5	1,975
Black	5.3	4.8	1,154

kees established their own households. Among the Senecas and Yakamas, a large percentage of married children lived with parents or in-laws. The percentage of married Senecas and Yakamas living with parents is especially high given that their low life expectancies would have minimized the opportunity to live with parents.

In general, tribes with the most complex household structure had the demographic regimes least favorable for population growth. The Yakamas had the most complex households, the highest mortality, and the lowest fertility, followed by the Senecas. The Cherokees had the least complex households, the lowest mortality, and the highest fertility. Although Seneca and Red Lake mortality levels were in the same range, the Red Lake Ojibways had higher fertility than the Senecas, and more households organized as nuclear families.

The relationship between fertility and household structure can also be examined within each tribe. Table 4.8 compares the mean number of own-children under five for women ages 15–44 and the proportion of children dead. For all five Indian groups, there was higher fertility in nuclear-family households; however, these fertility figures are unadjusted for mortality, which would account for apparent fertility differences between the two groups of Cherokees. Even considering the effects of mortality, for each of the other Indian groups' fertility was higher in nuclear-family households. The difference was most pronounced at Red Lake, where women living in nuclear families had very high fertility despite their higher mortality.

The causality between demography and household structure is unclear. High mortality could fragment nuclear families, forcing survivors to join other house-

TABLE 4.8

Fertility and Mortality by Household Type for Currently
Married (Spouse Present) Women, Ages 15–44, in 1900

	Proportion of Children Dead	Mean Own-Children Under Five (× 1,000)	N
Cherokee			
Nuclear family	.25	1,065	347
Extended family	.28	1,015	111
Seneca			
Nuclear family	.35	868	182
Extended family	.40	717	89
Red Lake			
Nuclear family	.40	1,008	108
Extended family	.31	783	38
Yakama			
Nuclear family	.38	869	106
Extended family	.47	585	128
Navajo			
Nuclear family	–	833	181
Extended family	–	751	68
White			
Nuclear family	.14	854	884
Extended family	.11	877	171
Black			
Nuclear family	.23	931	524
Extended family	.25	820	107

Note: Indian women includes non-Indian women with Indian spouses; figures for the Navajo proportion of children dead are excluded because they are based on retrospective responses (see chap. 3).

holds as extended relatives, or perhaps extended-family households had higher mortality because they created an environment conducive to the spread of infectious diseases such as tuberculosis. Extended-family households may have been more fluid in membership, with people moving in and out over periods of time. Also, extended-family households may have had fewer resources, and women making childbearing decisions may have practiced fertility control in response to recognizing the needs of people already in the household.

CONCLUSION

There is no single explanation for why these Indian tribes had different mortality, fertility, and rates of population increase. Because most theories tend to use Euro-American demographic experience as a standard or model, they offer little insight into differentials in Indian mortality and fertility at the turn of the century. Economics and culture were undoubtedly factors in determining Indian demographic patterns, but not in the ways suggested by demographic theories. Moreover, the generalizing intent of demographic theory obscures the particularities of the human experience, and in this case the particularities are important.

While all five tribes could be considered "premodern," "preindustrial," and "non-Western," the two tribes at opposite extremes in their familiarity and involvement with Euro-Americans had the demographic rates most favorable to population growth. It could be argued that the Cherokees rebounded from population loss so quickly because they became Westernized through intermarriage with whites, school education, and the development of a capitalist economic mentality. But the Navajos in 1900 were neither intermarrying with whites nor sending their children to school, nor in other contexts acquiring much knowledge of the English language or Anglo customs. Although they may have developed a culture that supported profit-maximizing behavior, they did so independently and not through assimilation of Euro-American economic values. Thus the key to a quick population recovery may have been to have a lot of contact with Euro-Americans—or as little as possible.

But even that would be too simple an explanation. Varying cultural traditions and responses to change influenced each tribe's rate of growth as they began to recover from population loss. The Cherokee Nation encouraged intermarriage through a liberal granting of citizenship to intermarried whites. The Senecas did not. The Cherokees and Navajos sanctioned the individual and family pursuit of wealth, which may have led to larger families, more laborers, and more economic security. Wealth was a contested issue within Cherokee and Navajo society, but more of their people accumulated wealth, either in land or herds, than among the Senecas, Red Lake Ojibways, or Yakamas. And although all tribes had traditions of extended-family households, those cultures with the most-complex households appear to have been hit hardest by Euro-American contact. In 1900 the highly extended Yakama and Seneca family households had fertility rates that could barely compensate for their mortality. In contrast, those cultures that had a predominantly nuclear-family household structure grew the fastest: the Cherokees, the Navajos, and then the Red Lake Ojibways.

CHAPTER FIVE

POSTSCRIPT TO RECOVERY

As discussed in chapter 1 and further demonstrated with the five population histories in chapter 2, the Indian population began a slow recovery around 1900. It was not until several decades later, however, that the population began to grow rapidly as life expectancy rose and Indian fertility remained high. This mid-twentieth-century spurt in Indian population growth occurred amid a larger social and political transformation. In 1900, most Indians lived in isolated Indian communities, but World War II ushered in a period of rapid integration into U.S. society. As Indians entered the mainstream, they became an economically disadvantaged minority group in addition to being a colonized people. Thus, from 1940 to 1980, there was rapid Indian population growth, but at what cost?

To assess the ambivalent consequences of integration, I have analyzed federal census data from the 1940 through 1980 *Public Use Samples* for Indians, whites, and blacks (see appendix). I first compared urbanization and education as indicators of increased integration. Second, I compared income and household structure to show how economic disadvantagement accompanied this process of integration. And third, I looked at two components of Indian population growth in the 1940–80 time period, intermarriage and fertility, and discuss the relationship between demography and Indians' changing social and economic status.[1]

INTEGRATION: URBANIZATION AND EDUCATION

There is a long history of Euro-American efforts to integrate, or assimilate, American Indians, but these efforts intensified in the late nineteenth century when the federal government developed a package of assimilationist policies, the most devastating of which proved to be land allotment and boarding schools. This campaign culminated in a 1924 law that made U.S. citizens of any Indians who had not yet become citizens by other means. When the Indian Citizenship Act went into effect, the vast majority of Indians lived on reservations or in other predominantly Indian communities; however, by the 1920s the number of Indians who had left their reservations was substantial enough for "migrated Indians" to merit an entire chapter in the landmark study of conditions among Indians known as the Meriam report.[2]

World War II initiated the first large-scale Indian migration away from reservations. Many Indian men went overseas to fight in the war, and many Indian women moved to cities to work in defense industries.[3] After the war, as part of a new wave of assimilationist policies, the federal government encouraged more urban migration by starting a relocation assistance program for Indians in 1952. About 100,000 Indians took advantage of Relocation's job placement and training services, but most Indians who moved to cities in the 1950s and afterward relied on their own resources.[4] Certain cities attracted large Indian populations. The Los Angeles-Long Beach metropolitan area, with fewer than 1,000 Indians in 1940, had 50,000 by 1980, making it the urban area with the most Indian residents. Cities in Arizona and Oklahoma, states with historically large Indian populations, also had many Indian residents, and the Twin Cities and Chicago, which drew Indians from the surrounding Midwest.[5]

Table 5.1—which gives figures on urbanization among Indians, whites, and blacks from 1940 to 1980—shows how quickly Indians became an urban population. The 1940 and 1950 censuses probably undercounted urban Indians because, before 1960, the U.S. census recorded race on the basis of enumerator observation. Enumerators not only may have had trouble identifying Indians as such, but they also may not have expected to find Indians in cities. For example, the 1950 federal census reported only 589 Indians living in Minneapolis-St. Paul in contrast to the several thousand Indians claimed as residents in local sources.[6] Also, the later censuses, which we know include many people who between censuses changed their identity to Indian, overstate the extent of urban migration. People who began asserting an Indian identity in 1970 and 1980 very likely lived off-reservation to begin with.[7] Thus the changes in census procedures and ethnic identity discussed in chapter 1 slightly exaggerate the rapidity of this urbanization.[8]

TABLE 5.1

Percentage of Indians, Whites, and Blacks Residing in
Urban Areas (places with 2,500 or more people), 1940–1980

	Indian	White	Black
1940	8.1	57.5	48.6
1950	16.3	64.3	62.4
1960	27.8	69.5	73.2
1970	44.9	72.4	81.3
1980	52.7	71.3	85.3

Sources: U.S. Census Bureau, *Sixteenth Census of the United States: 1940. Population*, vol. II, *Characteristics of the Population*, pt. 1, United States Summary (Washington, D.C: GPO, 1943), 20–21; U.S. Census Bureau, *Census of Population: 1950*, vol. II, *Characteristics of the Population*, pt. 1, United States Summary (Washington, D.C.: GPO, 1953), 88; U.S. Census Bureau, *U.S. Census of Population: 1960*, vol. I, *Characteristics of the Population*, United States Summary (Washington, D.C.: GPO, 1964), 144; U.S. Census Bureau, *Census of Population: 1970*, vol. I, *Characteristics of the Population*, pt. 1, United States Summary—Section 1 (Washington, D.C.: GPO, 1973), 262; U.S. Census Bureau, *1980 Census of Population*, vol. 1, chap. B, *General Population Characteristics*, pt. 1, United States Summary (Washington, D.C.: GPO, 1983), 20.

Despite these qualifiers, table 5.1 is useful for showing the general trend: all three groups became more urban between 1940 and 1980, with blacks overtaking whites as the most urban in 1960. The percentage of the Indian population residing in urban areas began increasing rapidly after 1940, and by 1980 more than half the Indian population in the United States lived in urban areas. Indian urbanization represents a dramatic change; however, in 1980 Indians were still one of the most rural subgroups of the U.S. population.

Indians also became more integrated with other Americans in the twentieth century through school education. Although missionary schools had operated since the seventeenth century, the federal government's boarding-school system, established in the 1880s at Carlisle and Hampton, was for most Indians their first exposure to school. The assault on Indian culture implemented in the curriculum of mission and BIA schools made many Indian students ambivalent about going to school. In the 1920s the federal government began advocating an on-reservation day-school system instead. With the Johnson-O'Malley Act in the 1930s, whereby the federal government reimbursed states for each Indian child enrolled in a public school, more Indian children began to attend off-reservation public schools, an experience that created further ambivalence. Since the 1960s an increasing number of tribes and urban Indian communities have developed their own schools and curriculums as a means to infuse tribal cultural content into a school education.[9]

TABLE 5.2

Education for Indians, Whites, and Blacks,
Ages 25–40, 1940–1980

	Indian		White		Black	
	Men	Women	Men	Women	Men	Women
Mean number of years in school						
1940	6.3	6.5	9.5	9.7	5.5	6.5
1950	8.6	8.8	11.8	11.9	8.8	9.6
1960	9.5	9.4	12.6	12.4	10.0	10.7
1970	12.1	11.8	14.5	14.1	12.4	12.8
1980	14.2	13.9	15.7	15.2	14.3	14.3
Percentage never attended						
1940	11.9	17.1	1.6	1.4	6.6	4.1
1950	9.0	12.7	0.7	0.6	2.1	1.1
1960	7.2	10.6	0.4	0.6	1.8	0.5
1970	3.8	5.5	0.4	0.5	1.2	1.0
1980	0.8	1.2	0.1	0.4	0.6	0.4
Number of cases						
1940	326	350	725	742	767	837
1950	368	386	830	863	829	932
1960	458	483	833	867	890	1,013
1970	692	707	804	827	964	1,143
1980	1,707	1,919	1,091	1,087	1,362	1,573

Note: In 1940 "years in school" is the number of completed years. For 1950 through 1980, "years in school" is the number of years attended. For the 1950 figures, I had to use the 1960 census and the 35–50 age group (see appendix).

Sources: 1940, 1960, 1970, 1980 public use samples.

Although historically Indians had a different relationship to school education than either whites or blacks, by 1980 they had attained educational levels equivalent to those of blacks and had significantly narrowed the gap between educated Indians and whites. Table 5.2 summarizes Indian, white, and black educational levels for one age cohort, 25 to 40 year olds, from 1940 to 1980. The most striking differences are evident for 1940 because a substantial number of Indians had never attended school. By 1980 school attendance had clearly become the norm for Indians, as it already was for blacks and whites. When education is measured as the mean number of years of school attendance, Indians and blacks had less education than whites in all years. While Indians and blacks in 1940 had slightly more than six years of schooling, whites had more than nine years, a gap of three years. By 1980 the gap between the two minority groups and whites was only about one year.

Even though urbanization and school education brought Indians into closer contact with non-Indians and the dominant culture, integration did not result in social equality. Indians arriving in cities from reservations often found themselves living in the poorest minority neighborhoods through the combined forces of housing discrimination and low incomes, and Indian access to education has always lagged behind that of whites.[10] Initially this lag was by design. Government boarding schools emphasized industrial education, prepared Indian men to work as farm laborers or as skilled laborers in carpentry or metalwork and trained Indian women to become housewives, which in the marketplace translated into domestic servitude.[11] By World War II the majority of most Indians went to school in the same facilities, with the same teachers and curriculums, as whites, but, as was also true of blacks, they did not stay in school as long as whites did.

ECONOMIC DISADVANTAGEMENT:
INCOME AND HOUSEHOLD STRUCTURE

That Indians were not fully integrated in American society by 1980 becomes more apparent by comparing income and poverty levels of Indians, whites, and blacks. Indians entered the mainstream only to be marginalized economically. As discussed in chapter 4, economic dependency was on the rise on most reservations in 1900, and many Indians could have been described as living in poverty even then. But poverty is relative and depends partly on one's standards and expectations. As also discussed in chapter 4, comparative poverty for different kinds of economies is difficult to measure.

Economic conditions on reservations did not improve much in the decades after 1900 and may even have become worse. The 1928 Meriam report cited Indian poverty as one of the major social problems facing government agencies responsible for Indian welfare. The report tabulated wealth and income for many tribes, and although unconvinced at the accuracy of their statistics, researchers could at least conclude that, for nearly every tribe, "The standard of living is almost unbelievably low" and many Indians lived on the edge of starvation.[12] The Meriam report also determined, with more certainty, that Indians were living in an economy that was different from that of other Americans since nearly all their quantifiable wealth was in land that was either unproductive or gener-

TABLE 5.3

Income for Indians, Whites, and Blacks in 1939

	Indian	White	Black
Percentage with $50 or more in nonwage income			
Men (18 years+)	46	33	30
Women (18 years+)	28	16	16
Percentage with wage income			
Men (18 years+)	53	67	65
Women (18 years+)	15	25	36
Median income per week for wage/salary earners			
Men ($)	58.78	119.60	52.26
Women ($)	51.00	78.39	24.15
Number of cases			
Men, 18 years+	887	2,085	1,850
wage/sal. earners	461	1,394	1,185
Women, 18 years+	881	2,077	2,044
wage/sal. earners	128	516	721

Note: These figures have been translated into 1979 dollars.

Source: 1940 public use sample.

ated income only by being leased or sold. In 1928, as in 1900, most Indians survived by a combination of traditional subsistence activities, leasing or annuity income, and sporadic wage income from occasional jobs as unskilled laborers.[13]

On the eve of World War II, Indians still lived in this quasi-separate economy. The 1940 census asked individuals for their total wage income in 1939 and whether individuals had received any nonwage income (for example, farm and business profits, leasing income, or old-age assistance).[14] Table 5.3, which lists responses to both these questions, shows that more Indians had nonwage income than whites or blacks, and that fewer Indians had wage income. While a few Indians were employed as professionals—doctors, teachers, nurses, and Indian office bureaucrats—most wage-earning Indians worked as farmhands, as seasonal farm laborers, or under the auspices of the Civilian Conservation Corps—Indian Division, a New Deal program that opened up wage-earning possibilities on many reservations.[15]

Table 5.3 also compares median weekly wages. Wage-earning Indian men made about the same pay as black men, and Indian women earned nearly as much as Indian men. Black women had strikingly low wages, perhaps because many were employed as live-in domestic servants, though this was also one of the few jobs available to Indian women. Whites made more money for a week's labor presumably because they held more skilled and professional jobs and because discrimination kept wages low for blacks and Indians. Minority status seems to have been an important factor in determining wages since Indian and black men earned only about half the wage paid to white men. However, as Gary Sandefur and Wilbur Scott discovered when comparing black and Indian wage earning using the 1976 *Survey of Income and Education,* social characteristics such as education explained the differences between Indian and white wages; that is, if Indian education levels and other social characteristics had matched those of whites, there would have been no difference in wages. But there was an unexplained factor for blacks, which indicates that they faced more discrimination than Indians in the job market.[16]

By 1979 wages and salaries had become the main source of income for most Indians.[17] As they became more dependent on wage income, Indians continued to have much lower incomes than whites. Table 5.4 presents figures on income for Indians, whites, and blacks in 1959, 1969, and 1979, measured as mean household income and per capita household income. Both Indians and blacks were at an economic disadvantage in all three years, with only slight gains apparent by 1979, when their per capita income was slightly more than half the per capita income of whites. Until 1979 Indians were the poorest of the three groups. Although 1969 total household income for Indians was higher than that for blacks, their larger families made for a lower per capita income.

Table 5.5 helps to further examine these differences by allowing comparison of the percentages of people living in poverty in 1979.[18] About one-third of Indians and blacks lived below the poverty line, compared to only about one of ten whites.[18] Much higher percentages of Indian and black children lived in poverty than white children. Blacks were the most likely to be living in poverty. Among married couples, however, Indians married to other Indians were by far the poorest. Indians married to non-Indians were much better off than blacks.

From 1940 to 1980 Indians became more integrated in the American economy as wage earners. At the same time Indians' economic situation, measured in terms of income, improved. The influx of people newly identifying as Indian helped to raise the average income level, but other factors such as more education and the migration from rural and reservation areas to cities also translated into higher incomes.[19] Despite the rise in their income levels, nearly one out of three Indians still lived below the poverty line in 1980, and just as Indians became more like other Americans in their dependence on wages for income, Indian poverty also came to resemble the poverty experience of other Americans.

TABLE 5.4
Income for Indians, Whites, and Blacks, 1959–1979

	Indian		White		Black	
	Total	Per Capita	Total	Per Capita	Total	Per Capita
Median household income (in 1,000s)						
1959	6.9	1.2	13.7	3.5	7.6	1.4
1969	11.2	2.1	18.5	4.6	11.0	2.3
1979	14.0	3.5	20.5	6.2	12.5	3.3
Percentage of whites' income						
1959	50	34	—	—	55	40
1969	61	46	—	—	59	50
1979	68	56	—	—	61	53
Number of cases						
1959	5,551		7,887		9,363	
1969	7,193		8,648		11,176	
1979	15,224		9,350		13,214	

Note: 1959 and 1969 figures have been translated into 1979 dollars; median household income is here defined as the combined income from all income sources for each household member age 15 and older.

Sources: 1960–1980 public use samples.

TABLE 5.5
Poverty Status, 1979

	Percentage Below Poverty Line	
	All Ages	Under 18
Indian	27.9	35.0
White	9.1	9.7
Black	30.2	38.5
Indians married to Indians	23.6	
Indians married to non-Indians	9.5	
Married whites	5.3	
Married blacks	15.9	

Number of Cases	Indian	White	Black
All ages	14,716	9,091	12,746
Under 18	5,654	2,444	4,624
Married	4,985	4,469	3,600

Source: 1980 public use sample.

FIGURE 5.1

Percentage of Individuals Living in
Extended-Family Households, 1940–1980

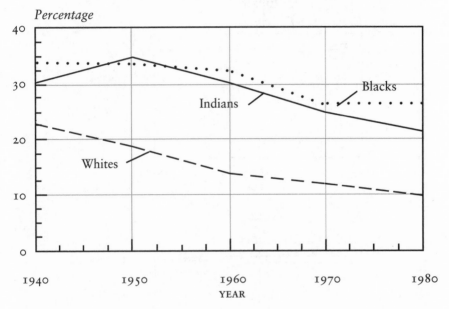

This becomes most apparent by comparing changes in household structure for the three groups.

Chapter 4 showed how, despite differences from tribe to tribe, Indians were more likely than whites or blacks to live in extended-family households in 1900. By 1980 the percentage of Indians living in extended-family households was rapidly declining. Comparing the percentage of individuals living in extended families reveals that from 1940 to 1980 Indians and blacks were more likely to live in extended families than whites, but all three groups experienced a steady decline in the number of people living in extended-family households (see figure 5.1).

At the same time the number of households headed by single mothers increased. Figure 5.2 graphically shows this trend by measuring the percentages of children living with neither parent, either parent (mother or father), and both parents. The percentage of children living with only their mothers increased in all three groups from 1960 to 1980. It was highest among blacks for the entire period, and second highest among Indians. Also, large percentages of Indian and black children lived with neither parent.[20]

FIGURE 5.2

Percentage of Children (Aged 10 and Under) Living with Both Parents, Mother Only, Father Only, or Neither Parent for Indians, Whites, and Blacks, 1940–1980

Indian

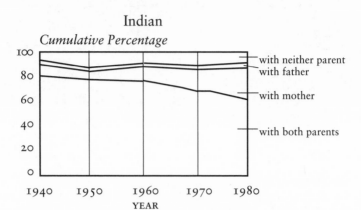

White

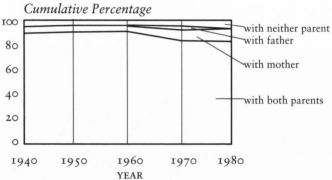

Black

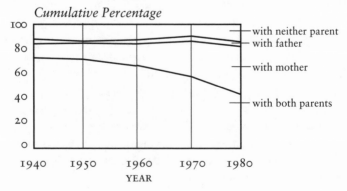

This sudden rise in single-parent families and female-headed households became the prime issue for policymakers and social analysts, who then investigated how this change in American family structure was both a cause and effect of poverty.[21] For Indians, the association between poverty and single motherhood was a recent development. Figure 5.3 compares the percentage of children residing only with their mother by income level. Dividing these three populations into four income groups was a difficult task given the disparity in income distribution. I arrived at the lowest income group by ensuring that at least 10 percent of whites fell into that category, and for the highest income group, I made sure that at least 10 percent of the minority populations qualified. Income here is measured as per capita household income. In these three graphs, covering three decades from 1960 to 1980, income is divided into four categories. In 1960 both blacks and whites had a large concentration of children living with just their mothers in the poorest income group. For Indians, income had little impact. Beginning in 1970 and especially in 1980, Indians shared in the same pattern as the other two groups. For all three groups, children living with just their mothers usually lived in poverty.

The sociologist Joseph Jorgensen and others who have researched or speculated on the relationship between poverty and the Indian family economy in the twentieth century argue that wage earning led to a transition to nuclear families and that the extended household was a sign of economic dependency.[22] Many Indians, however, had a cultural commitment to extended-family residence. In *Lakota Woman,* Mary Crow Dog described the continuing functions of the extended family, the *tiyospaye,* despite the burdens placed on it by the now dollar-driven reservation economy.

> Even now, among traditionals, as long as one person eats, all other
> relatives eat too. Nobody saves up money because there is always some
> poor relative saying, "Kanji, I need five bucks for food and gas," and he
> will not be refused as long as there is one single dollar left. Feeding
> every comer is still a sacred duty, and Sioux women seem always to be
> cooking from early morning until late at night. Fourth and fifth cousins
> still claim relationship and the privileges that go with it. Free enterprise
> has no future on the res.[23]

Like Jorgensen, Crow Dog equated extended families with poverty but explained it as resulting from adhering to traditional values of economic reciprocity among relatives. As figure 5.3 makes apparent, however, Indians searching for economic security through "free enterprise" would not necessarily have found themselves living in financial comfort as part of nuclear families; the Indian extended family has not been replaced by nuclear families, but by nuclear-family fragments.

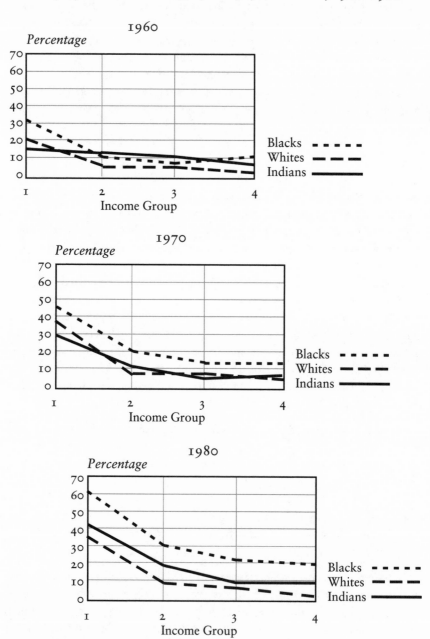

FIGURE 5.3

Percentage of Children (Aged 10 and Under) Living with Mother Only by Income for Indians, Whites, and Blacks, 1960–1980

I arrived at the lowest-income group by ensuring that at least 10% of whites fell into that category, and for the highest-income group, I made sure that at least 10% of the minority populations qualified. Income here is measured as per capita household income.

TABLE 5.6

Indian Intermarriage with Other Races, 1940–1980

| | Percentage of Currently Married Indians Married To | | | | |
	Indians	Whites	Blacks	Other	N
1940					
Men	87.8	11.8	.2	.2	528
Women	84.8	14.2	.7	.4	547
1950					
Men	88.6	9.6	1.3	.4	540
Women	85.8	13.5	.1	.5	558
1960					
Men	83.5	15.1	1.0	.4	777
Women	79.7	17.3	2.2	.7	814
1970					
Men	64.8	32.2	1.6	1.4	1,167
Women	60.2	36.7	1.8	1.2	1,255
1980					
Men	47.3	48.7	.8	3.2	2,456
Women	45.9	47.7	2.2	4.2	2,529

Sources: 1940–1980 public use samples.

COMPONENTS OF POPULATION GROWTH: INTERMARRIAGE AND FERTILITY

As discussed in chapter 4, Indians had been intermarrying with whites for centuries, but in 1970 and 1980 rates of Indian intermarriage with non-Indians skyrocketed (table 5.6). The 1980 census reported that more than half of married Indians were married to non-Indians. Several factors contributed to the surge in intermarriage rates in 1970 and 1980. First, the people who switched identities to Indian were probably not already married to an Indian. Also, as Indians moved away from predominantly Indian communities to urban areas, they would have been more likely to meet and associate with non-Indians than previously. In 1980, 60 percent of married Indians living in rural areas were married to other Indians; in contrast, 35 percent of married urban Indians were married to other Indians. As research on intermarriage for other ethnic groups has shown, small populations often marry outside the group because most of the people they know are of a different ethnicity or race.[24]

Turn-of-the-century policymakers believed that Indian intermarriage with whites would promote Indian assimilation, and that as whites absorbed Indians, Indians as a distinct race of people would die out.[25] Instead, intermarriage probably added to the Indian population by giving increasingly larger percentages of Americans some claim to an Indian heritage. However, tribal membership rules interacted with intermarriage to limit the number of Indians eligible for tribal enrollment. As the twentieth century progressed, most tribes came to rely on a particular "degree of Indian blood," usually one-fourth, to determine eligibility. Indians who are not members of tribes belong to a minority group but do not have the dual citizenship that comes with being a tribal member. Such high rates of intermarriage, without any changes in tribal enrollment rules, would make the self-identified Indian population grow faster than the Indian population as defined by the number of enrolled tribal members except for one additional factor: fertility.

The overview in chapter 1 of twentieth-century Indian fertility (based on analysis of aggregate published data) showed that by 1980 Indian fertility had become aligned with trends in white and black fertility, even though Indians still had more children. Data from the 1940–80 *Public Use Samples* allow for a more detailed look at this development, as well as the relationship between fertility and socioeconomic characteristics. To add precision to the basic fertility overview provided in chapter 1, table 5.7 compares fertility for all Indian, white, and black women, using the measure of own-children under five, from which I also derived total fertility rates (an estimate of the number of children a woman would have had by age forty-four if her experience summarized the fertility history of all women ages fifteen to forty-four).

As shown in table 5.7, Indian fertility was the highest of the three groups in all years. Black fertility was second highest in most years. All three groups experienced the baby boom, peaking in 1960, and the "baby bust" of the 1970s and 1980s. After the baby boom, Indian fertility declined dramatically to fall within the same general range as that for whites and blacks. Pinpointing the exact moment when the Indian population began its fertility transition is complicated by the baby boom's simultaneous occurrence. The extremely rapid fertility decline in the Indian population beginning in the 1970s had several causes: the secular fertility decline, the "baby bust" factors behind the post-baby-boom declines in white and black fertility, and the changes in ethnic identity and census procedures that brought more people into the Indian population after 1960.

The increase in intermarriage also contributed to the declining Indian fertility of 1970 and 1980. Figure 5.4 compares marital fertility to determine the effect of Indian intermarriage. After the baby boom Indians married to other Indians experienced a decline in fertility but still continued to have much higher fertility than Indians married to non-Indians, whites, and blacks. This reverses

TABLE 5.7

Fertility for Women, Ages 15–44, 1940–1980

	1940	1950	1960	1970	1980
Mean number of own-children under five					
Indian	.710	.762	.934	.516	.370
White	.309	.457	.623	.423	.283
Black	.348	.448	.652	.495	.315
Total fertility rate					
Indian	4.5	5.2	6.1	3.4	2.4
White	1.9	2.8	3.6	2.5	1.7
Black	2.3	3.0	4.4	3.2	2.2
Number of cases, Women 15–44					
Indian	716	680	1,007	1,624	3,961
White	1,455	1,519	1,576	1,840	2,103
Black	1,646	2,216	1,950	2,489	3,328

Note: These figures are adjusted for child mortality. The life expectancy rates from the Indian Health Service and other sources (provided in table 1.2) were the basis of reverse-surviving the number of children under five based on the model life tables in Ansley J. Coale and Paul Demeny, with Barbara Vaughan, *Regional Model Life Tables and Stable Populations*, 2nd ed. (New York: Academic Press, 1983). The 1940–1980 Indian mortality levels were based on Life Tables West Level 14 (1940), Level 18 (1950, 1960), Level 20 (1970), and Level 22 (1980); white mortality levels were derived from Life Tables West Level 19 (1940), Level 21 (1950), Level 22 (1960, 1970), Level 23 (1980); black mortality from Life Tables West Level 15 (1940), Level 18 (1950), Level 19 (1960, 1970), and Level 21 (1980).

Sources: 1940–1980 public use samples.

the pattern from earlier in the century of intermarried Indians having the highest fertility.[26] The reversal supports the probability that health and traditional customs restrained Indian fertility at the turn of the century. Later in the century fertility differentials had other causes.

Although the fertility of Indian couples remained high during the "baby bust," Indian fertility patterns came to closely resemble those of whites and blacks and fell subject to the same trends. Marital fertility measures, when applied to 1970 and 1980 data, miss a large portion of childbearing because more American women had children outside of marriage. The most dramatic change in childbearing patterns for Indians and other Americans since 1960 was in nonmarital fertility, especially among teenagers. Table 5.8 gives the percentage of infants under age one born to never-married mothers for 1940 to 1980 and the per-

Figure 5.4

Marital Fertility, 1940–1980

Mean Number of Own-Children Under Five

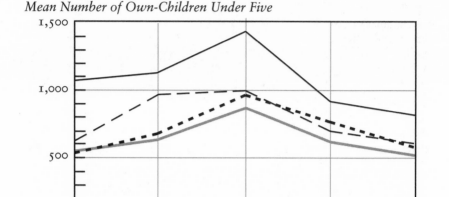

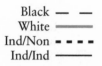

Black — —
White ▬▬▬
Ind/Non ▪ ▪ ▪ ▪
Ind/Ind ▬▬▬

Note: The "Ind/Ind" category refers to Indian women married to Indian men, and the "Ind/Non" category refers to intermarried Indian and non-Indian couples. These figures are the mean number of own-children under five for women 15–44, but unadjusted for mortality because I do not have precise information about mortality levels for children with two Indian parents versus children with one Indian parent and one non-Indian parent.

centage of young single women (ages fifteen to nineteen) who had had at least one child by 1970 and by 1980. The number of children born to never-married women increased, especially in 1970 and 1980, for all groups; however, differentials between groups were large. Never-married black women were more likely to have had children than Indian women, and more never-married Indian women had children than white women. Teenage black and Indian women were also much more likely than whites to have had children.

The age pattern of childbearing differed among these three groups at older ages as well. Figure 5.5 examines the age pattern of childbearing, the mean number of own children under five by the age of the mother, and shows how

TABLE 5.8

Childbearing Outside of Marriage, 1940–1980

	Indians	Whites	Blacks
Percentage of children under age 1 with never-married mothers			
1940	1.3	0.0	3.5
1950	0.0	0.0	2.2
1960	1.7	0.0	2.8
1970	3.3	1.4	22.4
1980	12.6	2.7	24.4
Percentage of never-married women, 15–19, who have had one or more children			
1970	8.9	1.4	13.2
1980	8.2	1.4	13.7
Number of cases children under age 1			
1940	75	77	86
1950	97	137	183
1960	175	181	246
1970	153	142	196
1980	317	146	221
Never-married women ages 15–19			
1970	360	365	546
1980	781	355	758

Note: Children under age 1 are limited to those living in the same households as their mothers.

Sources: 1940–1980 public use samples.

black and white women's fertility diverged in the years after the baby boom. The age pattern of Indian women's childbearing, though higher in nearly every age group in every year, became more similar to those of white and black women by 1970. However, at the same time, Indian women's experience came to be more like that of blacks. After the baby boom, while white women's childbearing began to concentrate around age twenty-five, Indian and black women were having more children at both younger and older ages. They started childbearing earlier and ended their childbearing later than white women.

In general, from 1940 to 1980, all three groups show a convergence in fertility patterns. Fertility differentials fell substantially, and all three groups experi-

FIGURE 5.5

Age Pattern of Childbearing
(Ages 15–44), 1940–1980

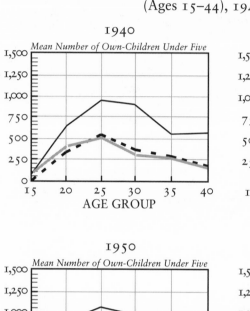

1940

Mean Number of Own-Children Under Five

AGE GROUP

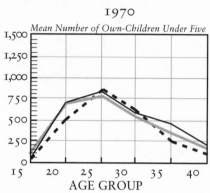

1970

Mean Number of Own-Children Under Five

AGE GROUP

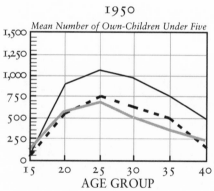

1950

Mean Number of Own-Children Under Five

AGE GROUP

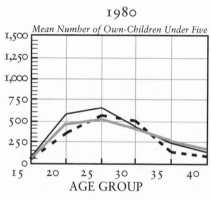

1980

Mean Number of Own-Children Under Five

AGE GROUP

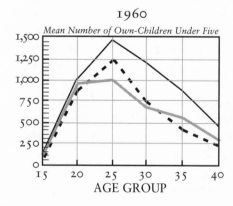

1960

Mean Number of Own-Children Under Five

AGE GROUP

—— Indian
- - - White
▬▬ Black

enced the same fertility trends. But there were some new and significant differences between black and white fertility apparent in 1970 and even more so in 1980: black fertility was now higher than white fertility; more black women had children outside of marriage, especially as teenagers; and black women had more children at older ages as well. As Indian fertility levels and patterns approached those for the other two groups, Indians fell somewhere in between, just as Indians by the end of the twentieth century were beginning to fall in between whites and blacks in terms of income and education.

Empirical studies have persistently found that more educated women have fewer children. Education could be considered both a cause and effect of demographic choices, for once women have children, pursuing an education becomes more difficult, and other women delay having children to pursue an education. Empirical research has been less successful at showing a consistent relationship between race, income, and fertility. Using data from the 1970 census, Rindfuss and Sweet found different relationships between fertility and income for different subgroups of the population. Those subgroups with higher incomes—urban whites, Chinese Americans, and Japanese Americans, for instance—had a positive relationship between income and fertility. Among rural blacks, Hispanics in the Southwest, and American Indians, fertility levels went down for the higher income groups. With data from the 1960 and 1970 censuses, Bean and Wood arrived at a positive relationship between fertility and income, a negative relationship for blacks, and mixed results for Mexican Americans. Johnson and Lean, using the 1980 census, found white fertility positively related and no relationship between black fertility and income.[27]

Tables 5.9a, b, and c present results of a regression analysis used to examine the effects of race, education, and income on fertility for 1960, 1970, and 1980. This type of regression is called a multiple classification analysis (MCA).[28] It is the second column of figures, the adjusted deviation from the mean, that is most important, for these figures indicate what women's fertility would be when all the other factors are controlled. Essentially, the adjusted figures weigh the differing impacts of age, race, income, and education on fertility. For example, table 5.9a gives the grand mean in the upper left corner. This is the mean number of children under five born to all women (Indian, black, and white, ages fifteen to forty-four) in 1960. So, in 1960, Indian, white, and black women ages fifteen to forty-four had a mean of .629 children under five. The first column, the unadjusted deviation from the mean, shows how much the mean number of children for women in each category varies from the grand mean. In 1960 Indian women had .19 more children than the grand mean, which would add up to .648 children under five. When adjusted in the regression analysis (and, therefore, when the other variables of race, education, and income are controlled

TABLE 5.9A

Multiple Classification Analysis: Mean Number of Own-
Children Under Five, Controlling for Age, Race,
Years of School Attended, and Income, 1960

| Grand Mean   .629 | Deviation from the Mean | | N |
	Unadjusted	Adjusted	
Age			
15–19	−.51	−.52	871
20–24	.31	.31	754
25–29	.56	.56	732
30–34	.15	.16	724
35–39	−.09	−.09	749
40–44	−.36	−.35	681
Race			
Indian	.19	.18	988
White	−.06	−.03	1,576
Black	−.05	−.07	1,947
Years of school attended			
Through the 8th grade	.05	.05	1,231
9th through 12th	−.01	−.00	2,711
Some college	−.06	−.10	569
Household income per adult (1960 dollars)			
$0–900	−.01	−.01	1,186
$901–1,999	.05	.04	1,279
$2,000–3,249	.07	.03	1,171
$3,250+	−.16	−.10	875

Note: All variables are significant to at least the .01 level.

Source: 1960 public use sample.

for), Indian women had .18 more children than the grand mean. In other words, if Indian women had the same age structure, education levels, and income as white and black women, their fertility was still considerably higher. Race was an important factor in fertility differentials.

This series of three tables shows that racial differences became less important over time once differences in age, education, and income were taken into account. In 1960 Indian women had substantially more children than other women. Black women also had higher fertility than white women. In 1970 a similar

TABLE 5.9B

Multiple Classification Analysis: Mean Number of Own-
Children Under Five, Controlling for Age, Race,
Years of School Attended, and Income, 1970

Grand Mean .438	Deviation from the Mean		
	Unadjusted	Adjusted	N
Age			
15–19	−.33	−.35	1,335
20–24	.24	.24	1,116
25–29	.38	.39	984
30–34	.14	.14	789
35–39	−.10	−.10	741
40–44	−.29	−.29	809
Race			
Indian	.04	.02	1,561
White	−.05	−.02	1,790
Black	−.01	.00	2,423
Years of school attended			
Through the 8th grade	.01	.03	855
9th through 12th	.01	.02	3,996
Some college	−.04	−.12	923
Household income per adult (1970 dollars)			
$0–1,859	−.01	.01	1,387
$1,860–3,999	.04	.03	2,065
$4,000–6,249	.03	.02	1,445
$6,250+	−.10	−.13	877

Note: All variables except race are significant to at least the .0001 level; race is not significant
(significance=.3).

Source: 1970 public use sample.

pattern persisted; however, fertility levels were closer together, and the differences between racial groups were not strong enough to be significant at even the
.1 level. By 1980 black and white fertility—once controlled for age, education,
and income—were identical, and Indian fertility had decreased to nearly the
same levels.

Thus, after the baby boom, Indian fertility came to be more dependent on
social class than in the past. By 1980, income and education differences explained why Indians, blacks, and whites had different fertility. Indians and blacks

TABLE 5.9C

Multiple Classification Analysis: Mean Number of Own-
Children Under Five, Controlling for Age, Race,
Years of School Attended, and Income, 1980

Grand Mean .323	Deviation from the Mean		
	Unadjusted	Adjusted	N
Age			
15–19	−.24	−.27	2,076
20–24	.15	.16	1,934
25–29	.25	.26	1,700
30–34	.10	.11	1,544
35–39	−.13	−.12	1,133
40–44	−.23	−.24	1,005
Race			
Indian	.04	.03	3,961
White	−.04	−.02	2,103
Black	−.02	−.02	3,328
Years of school attended			
Through the 8th grade	.05	.11	573
9th through 12th	.01	.03	5,964
Some college	−.03	−.09	2,855
Household income per adult (1980 dollars)			
$0–3,153	.00	.01	1,916
$3,154–8,499	.03	.02	3,736
$8,500–14,004	.00	−.01	2,444
$14,005+	−.09	−.05	1,296

Note: All variables are significant to at least the .006 level.

Source: 1980 public use sample.

were higher-fertility populations primarily because larger percentages of Indians and blacks had low levels of income and education. The growing importance of education and income as determinants of fertility suggests that cultural differences became less important as the century progressed.

While social class had come to be the most important factor affecting fertility for all three groups, there was still a distinctive political and cultural dialogue about Indian women's fertility that may have influenced women's childbearing decisions. This was particularly so in the late 1960s and 1970s among Indian political activists who vilified the history of Indian-white relations as genocide and self-consciously promoted pronatalism.[29] At about the same time, wanton sterilization by the Indian Health Service (IHS) became public knowledge, and this contemporary example of a government policy to limit Indian population growth added fuel to Indian activists' pronatalist rhetoric.[30] How many Indian women had children for what might be termed political reasons would be very difficult to measure. Studies of birth control use, conducted primarily among women living on reservations, usually cited ignorance or family intervention as the reasons why contraceptives found little favor in those communities.[31] However, this sociological research rarely considered the ways in which population control translates into political control.[32] If Indian women chose to have children in part for political reasons, to sustain a growing population, it may have compensated for women whose childbearing was cut short by sterilization policies common in the 1960s and 1970s.

CONCLUSION

From 1940 to 1980, American Indians became more integrated in American society than they were in 1900. They moved to cities, went to school, and earned wages. The increased involvement with non-Indians transformed Indians into a minority group; although Indian access to education and wage income had improved substantially by 1980, they still lagged behind whites and, as among blacks, nearly one out of three Indians lived below the poverty line. Changes in the Indian family reflected this economic disadvantagement as Indian households fell into step with the larger trend in American society: the rise in single-parent households headed mostly by women. Since 1960 American poverty has been typified by the growth of these kinds of households.

American Indians also experienced a demographic transition from 1940 to 1980. Life expectancy doubled, and fertility declined to become only slightly higher than white and black fertility levels. Dramatic changes in fertility occurred for all groups after the baby boom, after which Indian fertility began to follow the same trends found among whites and blacks. The higher Indian and black fertility in 1970 and 1980 can be explained by differences in social class. Race as a distinct variable does not explain the fertility differentials. However, race remained an obvious influence on social class (placing larger percentages of blacks and Indians at the bottom rung of the economy) and thereby indirectly affected fertility. Indian intermarriage with non-Indians, mostly whites, accelerated the process of Indians entering the mainstream but lessened the impact of minority status. Intermarried Indians were better off economically than Indians married to other Indians, but because intermarried Indians had lower fertility, people born of two Indian parents are the fastest-growing segment of the Indian population.

That Indians have come to resemble other groups of the U.S. population in their socioeconomic situations and family and demographic characteristics is an issue of great concern to Indian communities, which are currently struggling to create a space for Indian languages and traditions to continue living or to live again. The political activism of the 1970s inspired a cultural and political renewal in the midst of rising homogeneity, offering testimony to the power of identity to shape who people are.

CHAPTER SIX

CONCLUSION

Whenever I mentioned to people that I was working on a research project in American Indian population history, the standard response was, "And so what was the Indian population in 1492?" By the time I was nearing completion of the project, I had come up with a standard answer: "I don't know, but today there are about two million Indians in the United States." The Indian population recovery is the most significant demographic development of the twentieth century.

As this book has shown, the Indian recovery had a complex history with many causes and many consequences. The recovery can be dated to 1900, but rather than being an "event," it was a process with several stages. The initial catastrophic decline was followed by a period of stability or slow growth, which was in turn followed in the mid-twentieth century by a period of rapid growth. European diseases, primarily smallpox, and removal policies caused the most severe initial population declines. Yet, in the late nineteenth century, as the threat from sudden, epidemic disease diminished, and the federal government stopped removing entire tribes, the Indian population did not spontaneously rebound. Chronic diseases, particularly tuberculosis, continued to cause especially high mortality among Indians and also kept fertility down. Although Indian fertility was higher than that for whites and blacks in 1900, Indian marriage patterns (an early age at marriage and nearly universal marriage among women) should have led to much higher fertility and a faster growth rate. Not until after World War II did the Indian population fully embark on the road to recovery. Then Indian life-expectancy rates rose quickly while, at the same time, Indian fertility rates nearly doubled as Indians joined in the postwar baby boom.

To generalize more about the causes of the initial turnaround in the Indian population in 1900 would do an injustice to the variety of experiences across tribes. All native responses to this population crisis cannot be captured by comparing the history of just five tribes, but the differences and similarities between the Senecas, Cherokees, Red Lake Ojibways, Yakamas, and Navajos hint at some of the factors that had an impact on demographic rates and population growth. The Cherokees and Navajos grew the fastest. They had the highest effective fertility, with more of their children surviving to adulthood than in the other three tribes. In 1900, the Cherokees, in particular, had the mortality and fertility rates most likely to promote rapid population increase. The Cherokees also had high rates of intermarriage with whites, as well as liberal policies for incorporating the children of intermarried Cherokees as citizens. At the other extreme, the Senecas and Yakamas in 1900 had minimal growth rates, as indicated by their population histories and by analysis of their mortality and fertility. Although the Red Lake Ojibways had high fertility, nearly as high as Cherokee fertility, their mortality was more in the range of the Senecas', which slowed population growth at Red Lake.

Surprisingly, the most obvious differences between tribes had the least effect on how quickly they recovered from population loss. Those tribes with the longest, closest contact with Euro-Americans, the Senecas and Cherokees, were at opposite extremes in their demographic rates, even though they also had similar economies: a historical reliance on corn and later involvement in a regional agricultural economy dominated by Euro-Americans. Also sharing rapid rates of population increase were the most acculturated to Western values (the Cherokees) and the least acculturated (the Navajos), though both tribes suffered periodic setbacks caused by removal and other crises. Thus the type of economy, length of contact, and apparent acculturation had little bearing on how quickly a tribe recovered from population loss. Instead, differing growth rates had a variety of explanations, some of which reflect characteristics that the Cherokees and Navajos did have in common.

First, even though tuberculosis had become the leading cause of death among all Indians by the twentieth century, the Cherokees and Navajos had relatively low rates of infection. Tuberculosis also caused sterility and miscarriages. Therefore, not only did tuberculosis lead to high mortality, but it also lowered fertility. Through extensive intermarriage with whites, the Cherokees may have incidentally acquired resistance to tuberculosis. The Navajos had almost no intermarriage with whites, but their dispersed residence patterns, necessitated in part by an economy grounded in sheepherding, helped quell the spread of disease.

Disease was an important influence on demography, but not all tribes responded to it in the same way. Red Lake Reservation had high mortality levels, which confirmed contemporary reports that they had a high incidence of tuberculosis. And yet at Red Lake, fertility was nearly as high as Cherokee fertility. Red Lake fertility compensated somewhat for their high mortality, but their effective fertility and rate of population increase were still lower than those of the Navajos and Cherokees. Yakama and Seneca fertility barely compensated for their high mortality, but there is no indication that their disease environment was worse than at Red Lake. Disease alone is an insufficient explanation for varying demographic patterns among different tribes.

A second source of difference among tribes was the family economy. The Cherokees and Navajos had very different kinds of economies, but within both cultures large families may have been viewed as a path toward success and well-being. Both Cherokee and Navajo cultural values allowed for individuals to accumulate wealth. Like the Yakamas, Indians at Red Lake in 1900 were still trying to live by traditional hunting and gathering activities, though their activities were now oriented partly toward exchange in the Euro-American market economy. In contrast, the Cherokees and Navajos had, respectively, farms and herds for children to tend, and many aspired to make those farms and herds larger.

The third significant source of difference among these five tribes was household structure. In these five tribes, and as has been found in other empirical studies of household type and fertility, women living in nuclear families had more children than women living in extended families. Extended relatives probably do not insist that more children be added to the household, as some theorists have argued, but instead get in the way of procreation. Their presence might also indicate a reciprocal economy in which a large pool of relatives shares food and labor, in contrast to an economy in which the household accumulates and distributes wealth from parents to children or vice versa.

Little is known about Indian household structure before the reservation era, and thus far there have been surprisingly few investigations into Indian family history. Consequently, whether the differences between these tribes, as evident on the 1900 census, reflect traditional cultural values or adaptation to increasingly impoverished reservation economies is difficult to determine. The two tribes with the most-complex households in 1900, the Senecas and Yakamas, had a history of extended-family living arrangements. They also had the highest mortality and the lowest fertility. Indian tribes with a predominantly nuclear-family residence pattern at the time of European contact may have more readily survived the demographic collapse.

Demographers have theorized that the motors driving demographic change are "modernization," "industrialization," and "Westernization." This intellectual scheme for understanding demographic behavior unfortunately lumps Indians (and other peoples) together and presumes that nonmodern, non-Western peoples, essentially "others," must have the same family and demographic characteristics as each other, and that those characteristics must be opposite to those found in the "modern," "industrial" West. From "heterogeneity" to "homogenization" would be a better model. Indians did experience a demographic transition in the twentieth century, akin to what other Americans experienced a hundred or fifty years earlier. But the diversity apparent in 1900—diversity between Indians, whites, and blacks, as well as between Indian tribes—faded in the postwar period as demographic and family characteristics came to depend on and reflect social class much more so than race and ethnicity.

The three stages of decline, slow recovery, and population boom are not the end of the story. A period of slower demographic growth is in the offing. Although Indian life expectancy had increased substantially by 1980, Indian fertility had dropped even more precipitously. Two opposite forces worked to create the demographic and family patterns that have prevailed among Indians since 1960. Much of the recent growth in the Indian population resulted from people switching to an Indian identity. Because these newly identified Indians probably previously identified as "white," they brought their socioeconomic and demographic characteristics with them, thereby raising the average Indian income and lowering Indian fertility. Married couples who were both Indian, however, had higher fertility than intermarried Indian and non-Indian couples, which means that natural increase will continue to be a significant factor in Indian population growth. Indians married to other Indians were also more likely to be poor than Indians married to whites, married whites, and married blacks. Thus the fastest growing families within the Indian population as of 1980 were also the poorest. Add to this the post-1960 phenomenon of large percentages of children growing up in poor, female-headed households, and it is clear that poverty will continue to be a problem facing many Indian families.

As do other minority groups, Indians worry about the size of their population. Indian activists of the 1970s articulated their concern by taking a pronatalist stance. Indians have also taken other steps to ensure that their population will grow. Frustrated by the high rates at which Indian children were being taken from families and tribal communities and placed in foster homes or adopted, usually to live with non-Indian parents, Indian leaders lobbied for passage of the Indian Child Welfare Act (ICWA) in 1978. The ICWA gave tribes a legal role in locating homes for Indian children, and although many Indian children still fall through the loopholes, tribes have managed to keep more of their children within the community than before the ICWA.[1]

The desire to maintain a growing population, although a widely shared objective among many Indians, has also been a source of contention as tribes struggle to arrive at meaningful criteria for tribal membership. With more people wishing to be acknowledged as Indian, tribal enrollment review committees have been swamped with applications and inquiries. The lure of casino wealth and per capita payments (often exaggerated by the media, which focus on those tribes receiving the largest payments) has made the tribal enrollment issue especially pressing and divisive. Because most tribes still function primarily on funding from the Bureau of Indian Affairs and other government agencies, some tribes have been tempted to ease the enrollment requirements, for the larger the tribe, the greater the access to federal grants, made especially competitive by the shrinking federal budget for social programs. With such high rates of intermarriage, tribes with blood-quantum enrollment rules must anticipate either a smaller tribe or changing the rules. For a variety of reasons, some tribes have voted to change their enrollment requirements to enlarge the size of their tribe; others have changed the rules to restrict the number of members. All tribes are discussing the issue.[2]

For large minority groups, such as blacks or Hispanics, population can translate into real political power through voting. The Indian population will never be large enough to make them an identifiable voting bloc or to give them voice in most elections. Indians have fought for the right to vote and have organized their communities as voters, and in smaller elections in the northern plains or in the Southwest, Indian votes can determine an election. But numbering less than 1 percent of the total U.S. population weakens the potential for political clout as combinations of individuals. Real political power resides in the tribe.[3]

For Indians, the issue of population is less politically empowering than emotionally empowering because of the uniqueness of their population history. With European diseases and dispossession of their lands and way of life, Indians came close to not surviving as a people. But they have survived and, indeed, with a current population of two million, are no longer at risk of being remembered in history as the "vanished" Indians.

DATA

The data analysis for this book used primarily two types of U.S. census data. First, individual-level census data, which I collected from the microfilmed copies of the 1900 federal census manuscript forms, provided the basis for the comparison of five tribes. Second, I drew data from the 1940 through 1980 *U.S. Census Public Use Samples* to describe recent trends for all Indians in the United States and for whites and blacks. These public use samples are available from the Inter-University Consortium for Political and Social Research (ICPSR) at the University of Michigan. (Note that ICPSR is not accountable for what I have chosen to do with the samples.)

There are other public use samples available, and even others that will be available soon. For various reasons, these other public use samples were not suitable for this study. The 1900 and 1910 public use samples sampled a relatively small percentage of the U.S. population, which in combination with the small size of the Indian population made for few Indians (274 Indians in the 1900 sample and 1,168 in the 1910 sample). I do use data for whites and blacks from the 1900 public use sample to provide a larger context.

1900 U.S. CENSUS DATA

The 1900 federal census manuscript forms constitute the earliest available resource for microdata on all Indians in the United States. Earlier censuses were conducted among particular tribes to fulfill different purposes; for tribes that experienced removal, for example, there are usually censuses listing property and improvements. From the 1880s through the 1930s, Bureau of Indian Affairs (BIA) agents maintained enrollment lists for Indians on most reservations.[1] Although generally excluded from state jurisdiction, state censuses also sometimes included Indians. New York State enumerated Indians in its 1845, 1855, 1865, 1875, 1915, and 1925 censuses. Unfortunately, only the 1845 census, which is a household-level census, and the 1915 and 1925 census manuscript schedules for New York State Indians have survived.[2]

It was not until 1890 that the federal government enumerated the entire U.S. Indian population in the regular decennial census. In stipulating a decennial census, the original U.S. Constitution excluded "Indians Not Taxed" from the official U.S. population. "Taxed Indians" (Indians who were not living in recognized Indian communities, on a reservation, or in the as yet "unsettled" American West) were first enumerated in the regular federal census in 1850. Albert L. Hurtado's research on Indians in California shows some of the dangers in using federal census data for Indians before 1900. He analyzed data on Indians from the 1860 federal census and found extraordinary male-female sex ratios (considerably more men than women). The only explanation for this, he concluded, was rape, a crime which hurts women more than men (but which, however, does not necessarily lead to devastatingly high mortality for women). The other, more plausible explanation is that the pattern he found reflects the data collection process. Indians living on reservations and in other recognized Indian communities were excluded from the enumeration because they were "Indians Not Taxed." Women probably outnumbered men in California Indian communities in 1860, but the 1860 census did not enumerate them. Moreover, demographic studies of migration have shown that young, single men are usually the first to migrate. Hurtado should not have asked "Why are there so few women in the census?" when the best question was "Why are there so many men?"[3]

In 1880 the federal government edged toward including Indians in the decennial censuses by taking special censuses on several reservations, including the Yakama Reservation, using a specially prepared Indian form.[4] Finally, in accord with the government's drive for Indian assimilation, the 1890 census enumerated all Indians in the United States, whether they were "Indians Taxed" or "Indians Not Taxed." Unfortunately, nearly all the 1890 census manuscript forms were burned to free up storage space. The Census Bureau did, however, publish a massive report called *Indians Taxed and Indians Not Taxed,* which analyzed and tabulated some of the 1890 data.

I collected five data sets from the 1900 U.S. census manuscript forms, which are in National Archives microfilm collection T623. The following list gives the specific location of each data set.

1. Cherokees: "The Cherokee Nation," Indian Territory, reels 1843–46.
2. Seneca Nation: Cattaraugus and Allegany Reservations in Erie and Cattaraugus Counties, New York State, reels 1011, 1034.
3. Red Lake Ojibways: Red Lake Reservation, Minnesota, reel 756.
4. Yakamas: Yakima Reservation, Washington State, reel 1754.
5. Navajos: Navajo Indian Reservation, Moqui [Hopi] Indian Reservation (Navajos only), Arizona, reels 48 and 46.

The Seneca, Red Lake, and Yakama Reservation populations, all numbering one thousand to two thousand people, were a good size for data analysis, so for these tribes, I collected data for the entire reservation, excluding institutions and entirely non-Indian dwellings. The Seneca data consist of every dwelling with at least one Indian, excluding the Thomas Indian Orphan Asylum, which served all New York State Indians. The Yakama and Red Lake Ojibway samples are also complete populations of every dwelling with at least one Indian resident.

Because of the large size of the Cherokee and Navajo populations, I took a sample. For my sampling unit I used "dwelling," which the 1900 census instructions to enumerators defined as each building with a front door where at least one person slept.[5] The Cherokee data consist of a one-in-eight sample of every dwelling in the Cherokee Nation with at least one Indian. The Navajo data are a one-in-four dwelling sample. For the two sampled populations, the Cherokees and the Navajos, I entered every eighth and fourth dwelling, respectively, under the assumption that there would no systematic bias and to ensure that every neighborhood was represented proportionately.

Table A.1 gives the number of cases in each of the five data sets and the number of people racially identified as Indian. Except for the Cherokees, the data sets range from 1,300 to 2,200 individuals. I deliberately aimed for a large sample of the Cherokees so that I could look at patterns of intermarriage and

TABLE A.1

1900 U.S. Census Data Sets for Each Tribe

	Total Number	Number of Indians
Seneca	2,017	1,982
Cherokee	3,845	3,137
Red Lake	1,346	1,338
Yakama	1,645	1,620
Navajo	2,077	2,076

fertility. The Cherokees in 1900 were diverse. They were not necessarily more diverse than the other four tribes, but their heterogeneity was of the sort the U.S. census could capture: occupational specialization, municipal divisions, and high rates of intermarriage with whites.

Despite any gaps and imprecisions in the data resulting from one culture faced with having to answer another culture's questions, 1900 census data for Indians meet modern standards. Enumerators on Indian reservations were usually mixed-blood Indians, white men married to Indian women, or BIA employees. Their familiarity with the language and culture of the communities they were enumerating minimized the potential for misunderstandings, and interpreters accompanied enumerators who could not speak a language common to their enumeration area.

The 1890, 1900, and 1910 censuses had special forms for enumerating Indians. Along with the questions asked on the regular form, enumerators asked Indians a series of supplemental questions. In 1900 these extra questions were about the individual's tribe, father's tribe, mother's tribe, degree of white blood, type of dwelling (fixed or movable), whether "this Indian was" living in polygamy, whether taxed, and whether a citizen by allotment (i.e., whether an individual had become a U.S. citizen by receiving an allotment of reservation lands).

For this study it is the regular (nonsupplemental) variables in the 1900 and 1910 censuses that are especially important: age, sex, marital status, and the individual's relationship to the head of the household. These two censuses also asked women how many children they had ever had and how many were still surviving. The availability of the children-ever-born variable enhances fertility analysis, while the children-surviving variable allows for mortality analysis.

Because of the cultural differences implicit in the collection of this data, certain kinds of historical analyses would be of questionable utility. For example, the listed household head cannot be used as an indicator of status and authority. Enumerators showed their own biases by preferring 30- to 50-year-old males as household heads. Married women were frequently listed as heads but were either scratched out or placed lower in the household with arrows, probably after the enumerator discovered a husband living with them. The census also asked for the number of years married, but the responses are often contradictory or appear in very round figures.

This "age heaping"—the bulge of people listed with ages ending in round numbers—presents the biggest problem. Figure A.1 compares age distributions, from age 0 to age 55, for U.S. whites in 1900 and for the five Indian groups in my study. Some of the unevenness of these age distributions, particularly among the Red Lake Ojibways, is due to the small size of the data sets; however, most of the unevenness is due to age heaping, which is evident in each group's age

Age Distributions, 1900

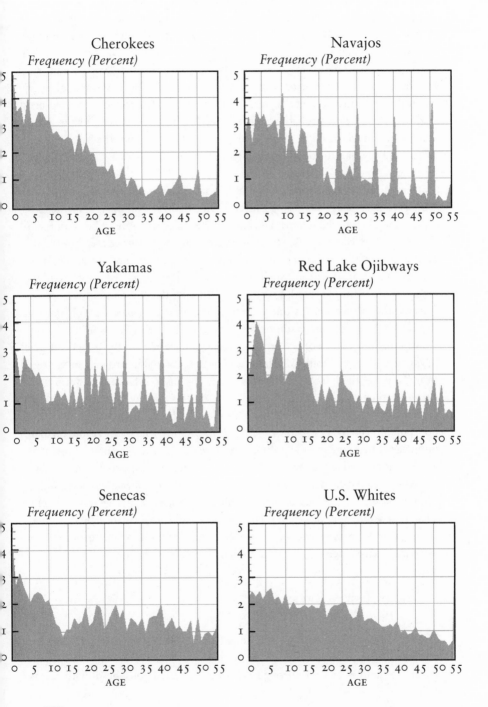

distribution. For the U.S. white population, there is clear age heaping at ages 20, 30, 40, 45, and 50. The Cherokees, Ojibways, and Senecas also have some age heaping.

The data for the Yakamas and Navajos reveal a great deal of age heaping. Obviously the Navajos and Yakamas did not keep track of ages in years, and most ages had to be estimated. One enumerator among the Navajo admitted that the ages listed were gross estimates but defended them as the ages given by the Indians themselves. The Senecas, Ojibways, and Cherokees recorded ages with more accuracy, probably because they had had more exposure to Euro-American culture through intermarriage and schooling than the Yakamas and Navajos. They had to some degree adopted the Euro-American tradition of recording ages.

Demographers can work around age heaping somewhat. By grouping individuals in age groups centering on the round figures—38–42 years instead of 35–39 and 40–44—people who estimated their ages will at least be captured in the correct age category. But there is a disadvantage to this strategy. Most demographers, out of habit and their own preference for round figures, use 5- or 10-year age groupings that break at 0 or 5. If I were to use a different age grouping from the standard, I would be hindering the comparability of my results to other researchers'. Consequently, I have opted for comparability and, in most cases, use the more traditional age categories (0–4, 5–9, etc.).

Although the choice of age group can have some effect on the final result, the advantage of comparability often outweighs the minimal improvement in precision. To judge the impact of different age groupings on the final result, I compared singulate mean age at marriage for the Navajos when grouped in the standard five-year age groups of 0–4, 5–9, and so on, and when grouped in the nonstandard groups of 0–7, 8–12, 13–17, and so on.[7] The method for singulate mean age at marriage gives an average age at marriage when the only information available is age and marital status. For Navajo women in 1900 grouped in standard age groups, singulate mean age at marriage was 18.0. For Navajo women grouped in 13–17, 18–22, 23–28 age groups, singulate mean age at marriage was 18.5, only a half year's difference despite the extreme age heaping in the data. The U.S. population, grouped in these two ways, showed no difference in singulate mean age at marriage, even though its age distribution had some age heaping.

PUBLIC USE SAMPLES

The public use samples for the decennial federal census vary in construction, in the size of the samples, and in what variables are available in each year.[8] I used the entire samples of 1940 through 1980 and extracted households with at least

Table a.2

Public Use Samples, 1900, 1910, 1940–1980

	Size of Sample	Number of Indians	Size of Subsample	
			Whites	Blacks
1900	1/760	274	1/7,600	1/1,520
1910	1/250	1,168	—	—
1940	1/100	3,618	1/2,000	1/2,000
1950	1/100	5,964	1/2,000	1/2,000
1960	1/100	5,551	1/10,000	1/2,000
1970	1/100	7,620	1/10,000	1/2,000
1980	1/100	13,000	1/10,000	1/2,000

Note: I used the "5% Sample" for 1970 and the "C Sample" for 1980.

one Indian resident. I used subsamples of the 1900 and 1940 through 1980 public use samples for comparative information on whites and blacks.

Table A.2 lists the proportion of the U.S. population in each of the public use samples, the number of Indians in each of the samples, and the size of the extracted subsample I used for comparative information on whites and blacks. The 1970 and 1980 public use samples are available in different forms. The 1940 and 1950 censuses asked special questions of people who happened to fall on a marked point on the census form. Because the public use samples only entered households containing one of these "sample-line persons," large households are more likely to be in the sample. In analyzing data from the 1940 and 1950 samples, a weight is used to adjust for the large households, and thus the number of cases appearing in any table in the text of this book is slightly smaller than the actual number of cases used. The number of Indians in the 1940 and 1950 public use samples listed below is the actual unweighted number of Indians in the sample.

As public use samples of the entire U.S. population, these samples do not have the specialized Indian questions sometimes asked in U.S. censuses. Information on an individual's tribe, for instance, is not available. Also, the 1940 and 1980 censuses rephrased questions, particularly those dealing with income and education, and asked different questions in different years. Similarly, there were changes in the methods used to construct the public use samples. For example, in 1950, income questions were on the "sample line," which means only one person in each household was asked questions about income. I did not use the sample line data for Indians in 1940 and 1950 because the samples were too small. Because the censuses and the public use samples were organized differently, the data analyses in chapter 5 often cannot span all five decades.

METHODS

Whether dealing with 1900 or 1940–80, wherever necessary the differing age structures of each population have been age-standardized to the 1910 U.S. population, an age structure that could be considered as falling in between the many different populations included in the data analysis.

NOTES

CHAPTER ONE

1. For an overview of the various estimates, see Russell Thornton, *American Indian Holocaust and Survival: A Population History Since 1492* (Norman: University of Oklahoma Press, 1987), 15–41; C. Matthew Snipp, *American Indians: The First of This Land* (New York: Russell Sage Foundation, 1989), 5–25; John D. Daniels, "The Indian Population of North America in 1492," *William and Mary Quarterly* 49 (1992): 298–320; William M. Denevan, ed., *The Native Population of the Americas in 1492* (Madison: University of Wisconsin Press, 1976); Henry F. Dobyns, *Native American Historical Demography: A Critical Bibliography* (Bloomington: Indiana University Press, 1976); Wilbur R. Jacobs, "The Tip of an Iceberg: Pre-Columbian Indian Demography and Some Implications for Revisionism," *William and Mary Quarterly* 31 (1974): 123–132.

For criticism of the methods and assumptions used by estimators of pre-Columbian population size see David Henige, "If Pigs Could Fly: Timucuan Population and Native American Historical Demography," *Journal of Interdisciplinary History* 16 (1986): 701–20; and David Henige, "On the Contact Population of Hispaniola: History as Higher Mathematics," *Hispanic American Historical Review* 58 (1978): 217–37. Also Henry Dobyns, Dean Snow, Kim Lanphear, and David Henige discuss precontact estimation in "Commentary on Native American Demography," in *Ethnohistory* 36 (1989): 285–307.

For more discussion on the impact of disease, see Alfred W. Crosby, Jr., *The Columbian Exchange: Biological and Cultural Consequences of 1492* (Westport, Conn.: Greenwood Press, 1972); Ann F. Ramenofsky, *Vectors of Death: The Archaeology of European Contact* (Albuquerque: University of New Mexico Press, 1987); John W. Verano and Douglas H. Ubelaker, *Disease and Demography in the Americas* (Washington, D.C.: Smithsonian Institution, 1992); and Clark Spencer Larsen and George R. Miller, ed., *In the Wake of Contact: Biological Responses to Conquest* (New York: Wiley-Liss, 1994).

2. This experience was not limited to the Americas. See, for instance, Ian Pool, *Te Iwi Maori: A New Zealand Population, Past, Present and Projected* (Auckland: Auckland University Press, 1991).

3. Sherburne F. Cook and Woodrow Borah, *Essays in Population History,* 2 vols. (Berkeley: University of California Press, 1971), 1:355, 376–410; 2:176; John Hemming, *Amazon Frontier: The Defeat of the Brazilian Indians* (Cambridge, Mass.: Harvard University Press, 1987); and Daniel T. Reff, *Disease, Depopulation, and Culture Change in Northwestern New Spain, 1518–1764* (Salt Lake City: University of Utah Press, 1991).

4. Alfred L. Kroeber, "Cultural and Natural Areas of Native North America," *American Archaeology and Ethnology* 38 (1939): 134; and James Mooney, "The Aboriginal Population of America North of Mexico," in *Smithsonian Miscellaneous Collections,* vol. 80, no. 7, ed. John R. Swanton (Washington, D.C.: Smithsonian Institution, 1928). Sixteen years earlier Mooney published a brief description of his population research and estimated that the indigenous North American population "at the time of the coming of the white man" was 1.15 million. James Mooney, "Population," in *Handbook of North American Indians North of Mexico,* ed. Frederick Webb Hodge, Smithsonian Institution, Bureau of American Ethnology Bulletin 30 (Washington, D.C.: GPO, 1912), 2:287.

5. Henry F. Dobyns, "Estimating Aboriginal American Population: An Appraisal of Techniques with a New Hemispheric Estimate," *Current Anthropology* 7 (1966): 395–416; and Henry F. Dobyns, *Their Number Become Thinned: Native American Population Dynamics in Eastern North America* (Knoxville: University of Tennessee Press, 1983).

6. Harold E. Driver, *Indians of North America,* 2d ed., rev. (Chicago: University of Chicago Press, 1969), 63; and Harold E. Driver, "On the Population Nadir of Indians in the United States," *Current Anthropology* 9 (1968): 330.

7. Russell Thornton and Joan Marsh-Thornton, "Estimating Prehistoric American Indian Population Size for United States Area: Implications of the Nineteenth Century Population Decline and Nadir," *American Journal of Physical Anthropology* 55 (1981): 47–53; Thornton, *American Indian Holocaust and Survival,* 30–32.

8. Douglas H. Ubelaker, "The Sources and Methodology for Mooney's Estimates of North American Indian Populations," in Denevan, *Native Population of the Americas in 1492,* 243–88; "Prehistoric New World Population Size: Historical Review and Current Appraisal of North American Estimates," *American Journal of Physical Anthropology* 45 (1976): 661–65; "North American Indian Population Size, A.D. 1500 to 1985," *American Journal of Physical Anthropology* 77 (1988): 289–94; and "North American Indian Population Size: Changing Perspectives," in Ubelaker, *Disease and Demography in the Americas,* 169–76.

9. Chapter 2 further explores the causes of depopulation for the Senecas, Cherokees, Ojibways, Yakamas, and Navajos. Other case studies of depopulation are Dean R. Snow and Kim M. Lanphear, "European Contact and Indian Depopulation in the Northeast: The Timing of the First Epidemics," *Ethnohistory* 35 (1988): 15–33; Emily J. Blasingham, "The Depopulation of the Illinois Indians," pt. 2, *Ethnohistory* 3 (1956): 361–412; Sherburne F. Cook, "Interracial Warfare and Population Decline Among the New England Indians," *Ethnohistory* 20 (1973): 1–24; Dobyns, *Their Number Become Thinned;* John C. Ewers, "The Influence of Epidemics on the Indian Populations and Cultures of Texas," *Plains Anthropologist* 18 (1973): 104–15; and Albert L. Hurtado, *Indian Survival on the California Frontier* (New Haven, Conn.: Yale University Press, 1988).

10. For a list of tribal "blood quantum" requirements, see Snipp, *American Indians,* 362–65. For more on census definitions and enumeration procedures, see Snipp, *American Indians,* 26–61; and Thornton, *American Indian Holocaust and Survival,* 186–224.

For the political and cultural context of the rise in people identifying as Indian since the 1960s, see Joane Nagel, *American Indian Ethnic Renewal: Red Power and the Resurgence of Identity and Culture* (New York: Oxford University Press, 1996). For more on the ambiguity of "Indian" as a racial, ethnic, or political category, see M. Annette Jaimes, "Federal Indian Identification Policy: A Usurpation of Indigenous Sovereignty in North America," in *Native Americans and Public Policy,* ed. Fremont J. Lyden and Lyman H. Legters (Pittsburgh, Pa.: University of Pittsburgh Press, 1992), 113–35; Ron Andrade, "Are Tribes Too Exclusive?" *American Indian Journal* 6 (1980): 12–13; Karen I. Blu, *The Lumbee Problem: The Making of an American Indian People* (Cambridge: Cambridge University Press, 1980); Susan Greenbaum, "What's in a Label? Identity Problems of Southern Indian Tribes," *Journal of Ethnic Studies* 19 (1991): 107–26; William T. Hagan, "Full Blood, Mixed Blood, Generic, and Ersatz: The Problem of Indian Identity," *Arizona and the West* 27 (1985): 309–26; and Ronald L. Trosper, "Native American Boundary Maintenance: The Flathead Indian Reservation, Montana, 1860–1970," *Ethnicity* 3 (1976): 256–74.

11. National Vital Statistics Division, "Matched Record Comparison of Birth Certificate and Census Information: United States, 1950," *Vital Statistics—Special Reports* 47, no. 12 (March 19, 1962): 368.

12. Jeffrey S. Passel, "Provisional Evaluation of the 1970 Census Count of American Indians," *Demography* 13 (1976): 397–409; and Jeffrey S. Passel and Patricia A. Berman, "Quality of 1980 Census Data for American Indians," *Social Biology* 33 (1986): 163–82. The 1990 census similarly showed an unusual increase but less extreme than in the previous two censuses. See David Harris, "The 1990 Census Count of American Indians: What Do the Numbers Really Mean?" *Social Science Quarterly* 75 (1994): 580–93. Also see Karl Eschbach, "Changing Identification Among American Indians and Alaska Natives," *Demography* 30 (1993): 635–51.

13. The percentage of Indian children with intermarried parents refers only to those children with both parents present in the household. This information is from the 1980 *U.S. Census Public Use Microdata Sample* (see the appendix).

14. Passel and Berman, "Quality of 1980 Census Data," 182.

15. Snipp, *American Indians,* 44–58; Or see the article version, "Who Are American Indians? Some Observations About the Perils and Pitfalls of Data for Race and Ethnicity," *Population Research and Policy Review* 5 (1986): 237–52. For more on how compositional changes in the Indian population affect demographic analysis, see Cary W. Meister, "The Misleading Nature of Data in the Bureau of the Census Subject Report on 1970 American Indian Population," *Indian Historian* 11 (1978): 12–19; Cary W. Meister, "Methods for Evaluating the Accuracy of Ethnohistorical Demographic Data on North American Indians: A Brief Assessment," *Ethnohistory* 27 (1980): 153–68; Ronald R. Rindfuss and James A. Sweet, *Postwar Fertility Trends and Differentials in the United States* (New York: Academic Press, 1977), 100–101; Gary D. Sandefur and Trudy McKinnell, "American Indian Intermarriage," *Social Science Research* 15 (1986): 347–71; Gary D. Sandefur and Arthur Sakamoto, "American Indian Household Structure and Income," *Demography* 25 (1988): 71–80; and Russell Thornton, Gary D. Sandefur, and C. Matthew Snipp, "A Research Note: American Indian Fertility Patterns: 1910 and 1940 to 1980," *American Indian Quarterly* 15 (1991): 359–67.

16. Karl Eschbach, "The Enduring and Vanishing American Indian: American Indian Population Growth and Intermarriage in 1900," *Ethnic and Racial Studies* 18 (1995): 89–108.

17. I started with the 1950 census population in five-year age groups (from U.S. Bureau of the Census, *U.S. Census of Population: 1950. Nonwhite Population by Race.* Special report, vol. 14, pt. 3, chap. B [Washington, D.C.: GPO, 1953], 60). I calculated the approximate number of newborns based on the child-woman ratios presented in figure 1.2 for 1955. I then subtracted the number of people in each age group who would have died by 1955 based on the life expectancy rates in table 1.2 and the appropriate life table from Ansley J. Coale and Paul Demeny, with Barbara Vaughan, *Regional Model Life Tables and Stable Populations,* 2d ed. (New York: Academic Press, 1983). I did each of these steps for every five-year period up to 1980.

18. For a discussion of factors contributing to compositional changes in the Indian population, see Thornton, *American Indian Holocaust and Survival,* chap. 8.

19. S. Ryan Johansson and S. Horrowitz, "Estimating Mortality in Skeletal Populations: The Influence of the Growth Rate on the Interpretation of Levels and Trends During the Transition to Agriculture," *American Journal of Physical Anthropology* 71 (1986): 233–50; and Kenneth M. Weiss, "Evolutionary Perspectives on Human Aging," in *Other Ways of Growing Old: Anthropological Perspectives,* ed. P. T. Amoss and Stevan Harrell (Stanford: Stanford University Press, 1981), 25–58; for a history of Indian mortality, pre-Columbian to the present, see S. Ryan Johansson, "The Demographic History of the Native Peoples of North America: A Selective Bibliography," *Yearbook of Physical Anthropology* 25 (1982): 133–52.

20. Lewis Meriam, *The Problem of Indian Administration* (Washington, D.C.: Institute for Government Research, 1928), 172, 196–201; Francis Paul Prucha, *The Great Father: The United States Government and the American Indians,* abridged ed. (Lincoln: University of Nebraska Press, 1986), 330–31, 353; Stephen J. Kunitz, "The History and Politics of U.S. Health Care Policy for American Indians and Alaskan Natives," *American Journal of Public Health* 86 (1996): 1464–73; and Todd Benson, "Race, Health, and Power: The Federal Government and American Indian Health, 1909–1955," Ph.D. diss., Stanford University, 1994. Clifford E. Trafzer in *Death Stalks the Yakama: Epidemiological-Nutritional Transitions and Mortality on the Yakama Indian Reservation, 1888–1964* (East Lansing: Michigan State University, 1997), 78–83, gives 1924 as the year when Bureau of Indian Affairs death reporting became systematic, at least on the Yakama Reservation. The Indian Health Service tends to give a more favorable assessment of Indian health than Indians themselves; see, for example, "Women of All Red Nations Respond to Official Government Report on Health Problems," *Lakota Times,* 18 Feb. 1982, 8.

21. Johansson, "Demographic History"; also see S. B. D. Aberle, "Child Mortality Among Pueblo Indians," *American Journal of Physical Anthropology* 16 (1932): 339–49; S. B. D. Aberle, "Maternal Mortality Among the Pueblos," *American Journal of Physical Anthropology* 18 (1934): 431–35; S. Ryan Johansson and S. H. Preston, "Tribal Demography: The Hopi and Navaho Populations as Seen Through Manuscripts from the 1900 U.S. Census," *Social Science History* 3 (1978): 1–33; Meriam, *Problem of Indian Administration,* chaps. 7 and 8; and Diane Therese Putney, "Fighting the Scourge: American Indian Morbidity and Federal Policy, 1897–1928," Ph.D. diss., Marquette University, 1980.

22. Passel and Berman, "Quality of 1980 Census Data," 168.

23. See, for example, Regina Kenen and Charles R. Hammerslough, "Reservation and Non-Reservation American Indian Mortality in 1970 and 1978," *Social Biology* 34 (1987): 26–36; and Cheryl Howard, *Navajo Tribal Demography, 1983–1986: A Comparative and Historical Perspective* (New York: Garland, 1993), 45–60.

24. Richard D. Kennedy and Roger E. Deapen, "Differences Between Oklahoma Indian Infant Mortality and Other Races," *Public Health Reports* 106 (1991): 97.

25. Ronet Bachman, *Death and Violence on the Reservation: Homicide, Family Violence, and Suicide in American Indian Populations* (New York: Auburn House, 1992); David W. Broudy and Philip A. May, "Demographic and Epidemiologic Transition Among the Navajo Indians," *Social Biology* 30 (1983): 1–16; Barbara A. Carr and Eun Sul Lee, "Navajo Tribal Mortality: A Life Table Analysis of the Leading Causes of Death," *Social Biology* 25 (1978): 279–87; and Robert A. Hackenberg and Mary M. Gallagher, "The Costs of Cultural Change: Accidental Injury and Modernization among the Papago Indians," *Human Organization* 31 (1972): 211–26.

26. See, for example, John Demos, *The Unredeemed Captive: A Family Story from Early America* (New York: Alfred A. Knopf, 1994), 157; and Joseph Francois Lafitau, *Customs of the American Indians Compared with the Customs of Primitive Times,* ed. and trans. William N. Fenton and Elizabeth L. Moore, 2 vols. (Toronto: Champlain Society, 1974–77), 1:591.

27. Wilson H. Grabill, Clyde V. Kiser, and Pascal K. Whelpton, *The Fertility of American Women* (New York: Wiley, 1958); and Ansley J. Coale and Melvin Zelnik, *New Estimates of Fertility and Population in the United States* (Princeton, N.J.: Princeton University Press, 1963); for more on the black fertility decline, see Stanley L. Engerman, "Changes in Black Fertility, 1880–1940," in *Family and Population in Nineteenth-Century America,* ed. Tamara K. Hareven and Maris A. Vinovskis (Princeton, N.J.: Princeton University Press, 1978), 126–53.

28. Since some children ages zero to four will have died before being counted in the census, child mortality affects child-woman ratios. Some mothers will have died also, but infant mortality is higher, making it more of a problem for this measure. Differential census undercount for women and children could also bias the results. Lacking the necessary information to adjust for child mortality and census undercount for the American Indian population, I have not made any adjustments. However, I did use indirect standardization to adjust for differing age structures between populations; see Henry S. Shryock and Jacob S. Siegel, *The Methods and Materials of Demography,* condensed ed. (San Diego: Academic Press, 1976), 242–44. I used the age-specific fertility rates of the 1910 U.S. population (derived from calculating mean own-children-under-five for women fifteen to forty-four in the 1910 Public Use Sample) as the standard. These standardized child-woman ratios, therefore, are the number of children under five for every thousand women *if* each population had the same age-specific fertility rates as the 1910 U.S. population.

29. Franklin B. Hough, *Census of the State of New York for 1865* (Albany: Charles Van Benthuysen and Sons, 1867), 604, gives age and sex breakdowns for New York State Indians for 1855 and 1865; for 1875, see Franklin B. Hough, *Census of the State of New York for 1875* (Albany: Charles Van Benthuysen and Sons, 1877), 196; and for 1930 see U.S. Bureau of the Census, *Fifteenth Census of the United States: 1930. The Indian Population of the United States and Alaska* (Washington, D.C.: GPO, 1937), 91.

30. Rindfuss and Sweet, *Postwar Fertility Trends,* examine minority-group differences during the baby boom in detail.

31. U.S. Bureau of the Census, *1980 Census of Population: Characteristics of the Population, United States Summary,* vol. 1, chap. B, pt. 1 (Washington, D.C.: GPO), 31–33; *1980 Census of Population,* vol. 2, *Subject Reports: American Indians, Eskimos, and Aleuts on Identified Reservations and in the Historic Areas of Oklahoma (Excluding Ur-*

banized Areas), pt. 2 (Washington, D.C.: GPO, 1986), 131; and Thornton, Sandefur, and Snipp, "Research Note," 363–64.

CHAPTER TWO

1. See, for instance, James H. Merrell, *The Indians' New World: Catawbas and Their Neighbors from European Contact Through the Era of Removal* (Chapel Hill: University of North Carolina Press, 1989); and Blu, *The Lumbee Problem*.

2. In my article "The Census as Civilizer: American Indian Household Structure in the 1900 and 1910 U.S. Censuses," *Historical Methods* 25 (1992): 4–11, I discuss in more detail the problems with BIA censuses and data collection procedures.

3. Daniel K. Richter, *The Ordeal of the Longhouse: The Peoples of the Iroquois League in the Era of European Colonization* (Chapel Hill: University of North Carolina Press, 1992), 17, 59–60, 65; Bruce G. Trigger, *The Children of Aataentsic: A History of the Huron People* (Montreal: McGill-Queen's University Press, 1976), 1:98; Dean R. Snow and William A. Starna, "Sixteenth-Century Depopulation: A View from the Mohawk Valley," *American Anthropologist* 91 (1989): 142–49; Gunther Michelson, "Iroquois Population Statistics," *Man in the Northeast* 14 (fall 1977): 3–17; and Thomas Donaldson, *The Six Nations of New York. Extra Census Bulletin: Indians* (Washington, D.C.: U.S. Census Printing Office, 1892), 2.

4. See Anthony F. C. Wallace, *The Death and Rebirth of the Seneca* (New York: Random House, 1969); and Barbara Graymont, *The Iroquois in the American Revolution* (Syracuse: Syracuse University Press, 1972).

5. Thomas S. Abler, "The Kansas Connection: The Seneca Nation and the Iroquois Confederacy Council," in *Extending the Rafters: Interdisciplinary Approaches to Iroquoian Studies*, ed. Michael K. Foster, Jack Campisi, and Marianne Mithun (Albany: State University of New York Press, 1984), 81–93; William C. Sturtevant, "Oklahoma Seneca-Cayuga," in *Northeast*, vol. 15 of *Handbook of North American Indians*, ed. Bruce G. Trigger (Washington, D.C.: Smithsonian Institution, 1978), 537–43; Thomas Abler, "Factional Dispute and Party Conflict in the Political System of the Seneca Nation, 1845–1895: An Ethnohistorical Analysis," Ph.D. diss., University of Toronto, 1969; and Christopher Vecsey and William A. Starna, ed., *Iroquois Land Claims* (Syracuse, N.Y.: Syracuse University Press, 1988).

6. Laurence M. Hauptman, *The Iroquois and the New Deal* (Syracuse, N.Y.: Syracuse University Press, 1981); Laurence M. Hauptman, *The Iroquois Struggle for Survival: World War II to Red Power* (Syracuse: Syracuse University Press, 1986); and Sharon O'Brien, *American Indian Tribal Governments* (Norman: University of Oklahoma Press, 1989).

7. Annual Report of the Commissioner of Indian Affairs (ARCIA) (Washington, D.C.: GPO, 1862, 1866, 1873, 1889); and Donaldson, *Six Nations of New York*, 2, 7.

8. Hough, *Census . . . 1855*, 500, 509; *Census . . . 1865*, 602; and Donaldson, *Six Nations of New York*, 6.

9. Hough, *Census . . . 1865*, 603.

10. Mooney, "Aboriginal Population," 8; and Peter H. Wood, "The Changing Population of the Colonial South: An Overview by Race and Region, 1685–1790," in *Powhatan's Mantle: Indians in the Colonial Southeast*, ed. Peter H. Wood, Gregory A.

Waselkov, and M. Thomas Hatley (Lincoln: University of Nebraska Press, 1989), 35–103, especially p. 63. For an evaluation of Mooney's versus Wood's estimates, see Russell Thornton, *The Cherokees: A Population History* (Lincoln: University of Nebraska Press, 1990), 15–18; and Charles Hudson, *The Southeastern Indians* (Knoxville: University of Tennessee Press, 1976), 97–119.

11. James Adair, *The History of the American Indians* (1775; reprint, New York: Johnson Reprint Corporation, 1968), 232–33.

12. James Mooney, *Historical Sketch of the Cherokee* (Chicago: Aldine Publishing Company, 1975) 29–53; Wood, "Changing Population."

13. William G. McLoughlin, *Cherokee Renascence in the New Republic* (Princeton, N.J.: Princeton University Press, 1986); William G. McLoughlin and Walter H. Conser, Jr., "The Cherokees in Transition: A Statistical Analysis of the Federal Cherokee Census of 1835," *Journal of American History* 64 (1977): 678–703; Theda Perdue, *Slavery and the Evolution of Cherokee Society, 1540–1866* (Knoxville: University of Tennessee Press, 1979); Rennard Strickland, *Fire and the Spirits: Cherokee Law from Clan to Court* (Norman: University of Oklahoma Press, 1975); and Thurman Wilkins, *Cherokee Tragedy: The Story of the Ridge Family and the Decimation of a People* (New York: Macmillan, 1970).

14. McLoughlin and Conser, "Cherokees in Transition," 681; Thornton, *The Cherokees*, 47; and Dianna Everett, *The Texas Cherokees: A People Between Two Fires, 1819–1840* (Norman: University of Oklahoma Press, 1990).

15. McLoughlin and Conser, "Cherokees in Transition," 681, 693.

16. Mooney, *Historical Sketch*, 111–43; Russell Thornton, "Cherokee Population Losses During the Trail of Tears: A New Perspective and a New Estimate," *Ethnohistory* 31 (1984): 289–300; and Morris L. Wardell, *A Political History of the Cherokee Nation, 1838–1907* (Norman: University of Oklahoma Press, 1938), 84.

17. ARCIA, 1859–1870; U.S. Senate, *Report of the Joint Special Committee on the Condition of the Indian Tribes*, J. R. Doolittle, Chairman, 39th Cong., 2d sess., 1867, S. Rept. 156, 441–42; and William G. McLoughlin, *After the Trail of Tears: The Cherokees' Struggle for Sovereignty, 1839–1880* (Chapel Hill: University of North Carolina Press, 1993).

18. Mooney, *Historical Sketch*, 143–60; McLoughlin, *After the Trail of Tears*, 222–88; and Daniel F. Littlefield, *The Cherokee Freedmen: From Emancipation to American Citizenship* (Westport, Conn.: Greenwood Press, 1978).

19. Angie Debo, *And Still the Waters Run: The Betrayal of the Five Civilized Tribes* (Princeton: Princeton University Press, 1940); Angie Debo, *The Five Civilized Tribes of Oklahoma: Report on Social and Economic Conditions* (Philadelphia: Indian Rights Association, 1951); and Muriel H. Wright, *A Guide to the Indian Tribes of Oklahoma* (Norman: University of Oklahoma Press, 1951).

20. The issue of growth rates after smallpox epidemics is discussed, with a series of simulations, in Russell Thornton, Tim Miller, and Jonathan Warren, "American Indian Population Recovery Following Smallpox Epidemics," *American Anthropologist* 93 (1991): 28–45.

21. R. Palmer Howard, "Cherokee History to 1840: A Medical View," *Oklahoma State Medical Association Journal* 63 (1970): 71–82.

22. Helen Hornbeck Tanner, ed., *Atlas of Great Lakes Indian History* (Norman: University of Oklahoma Press, 1987); William W. Warren, *History of the Ojibway People* (1885; reprint, St. Paul, Minnesota: Minnesota Historical Society Press, 1984); and Erminie Wheeler-Voegelin and Harold Hickerson, *The Red Lake and Pembina Chippewa*, vol. 1 of *Chippewa Indians* (New York: Garland, 1974).

23. Wheeler-Voegelin and Hickerson, *Red Lake and Pembina Chippewa,* 213.

24. Wheeler-Voegelin and Hickerson, *Red Lake and Pembina Chippewa;* Mitchell E. Rubinstein and Alan R. Woolworth, "The Dakota and Ojibway," in *They Chose Minnesota: A Survey of the State's Ethnic Groups,* ed. June Drenning Holmquist (St. Paul, Minnesota: Minnesota Historical Society, 1981), 17–35; Philip P. Mason, ed., *Schoolcraft's Expedition to Lake Itasca: The Discovery of the Source of the Mississippi* (East Lansing: Michigan State University Press, 1958); ARCIA, 1850–1907; and Melissa L. Meyer, *The White Earth Tragedy: Ethnicity and Dispossession at a Minnesota Anishinaabe Reservation, 1889–1920* (Lincoln: University of Nebraska Press, 1994).

25. Elizabeth Ebbott for the League of Women Voters of Minnesota, *Indians in Minnesota,* 4th ed., rev., ed. Judith Rosenblatt (Minneapolis: University of Minnesota Press, 1985); and Charles Brill, *Red Lake Nation: Portraits of Ojibway Life* (Minneapolis: University of Minnesota Press, 1992).

26. Brill, *Red Lake Nation,* 35.

27. Helen H. Schuster, *The Yakimas: A Critical Bibliography* (Bloomington: Indiana University Press, 1982); Helen H. Schuster, "Yakima Indian Traditionalism: A Study in Continuity and Change," Ph.D. diss., University of Washington, 1975; Eugene S. Hunn with James Selam and Family, *Nch'i-Wána, "The Big River": Mid-Columbia Indians and Their Land* (Seattle: University of Washington Press, 1990); Angelo Anastasio, "The Southern Plateau: An Ecological Analysis of Intergroup Relations," *Northwest Anthropological Research Notes* 6 (1972): 109–229; Gerald R. Desmond, *Gambling Among the Yakima,* Catholic University of American Anthropological Series, no. 14, Washington, D.C., 1952; Robert H. Ruby and John A. Brown, *Indians of the Pacific Northwest: A History* (Norman: University of Oklahoma Press, 1981); and H. G. Barnett, *The Yakima Indians in 1942* (Eugene, Ore.: Department of Anthropology, University of Oregon, 1969).

28. Elliott Coues, ed., *The History of the Lewis and Clark Expedition,* vol. 3 (1893; reprint, New York: Dover, n.d.), chap. 27; Anastasio, "The Southern Plateau," 202; Robert Thomas Boyd, "The Introduction of Infectious Diseases Among the Indians of the Pacific Northwest, 1774–1874," Ph.D. diss., University of Washington, 1985, 78–80, 101–2, 340, 352; and ARCIA, 1854.

29. Ruby and Brown, *Indians of the Pacific Northwest,* chaps. 13 and 14.

30. ARCIA, 1860, 1883.

31. ARCIA, 1881.

32. U.S. Census Office, *Report on Indians Taxed and Indians Not Taxed in the United States (Except Alaska) at the Eleventh Census: 1890* (Washington, D.C.: GPO, 1894), 614.

33. Lucullus V. McWhorter, *The Crime Against the Yakimas* (North Yakima, Wash.: Republic Print, 1913); Barbara Leibhardt, "Allotment Policy in an Incongruous Legal System: The Yakima Indian Nation as a Case Study, 1887–1934," *Agricultural History* 65 (1991): 78–103; and Schuster, "Yakima Indian Traditionalism," chaps. 3 and 4; Russell Jim's comments are quoted in Kenneth R. Philp, ed., *Indian Self-Rule: First-Hand Accounts of Indian-White Relations from Roosevelt to Reagan* (Salt Lake City: Institute of the American West, Howe Brothers, 1986), 106–8, 179–81, 254–55, 280–81.

34. Richard D. Daugherty, *The Yakima People* (Phoenix, Ariz.: Indian Tribal Series, 1973), 88.

35. Snipp, *American Indians,* 364.

36. Alonso de Benavides, *The Memorial of Fray Alonso de Benavides, 1630* (Albuquerque, N. Mex.: Horn and Wallace, 1965), 44; Denis Foster Johnston, *An Analysis of*

Sources of Information on the Population of the Navaho, Smithsonian Institution, Bureau of American Ethnology Bulletin 197 (Washington, D.C.: GPO, 1966), 20; and Donald E. Worcester, *The Apaches: Eagles of the Southwest* (Norman: University of Oklahoma Press, 1979), 10.

37. Ruth M. Underhill, *The Navajos* (Norman: University of Oklahoma Press, 1956); and Clyde Kluckhohn and Dorothea Leighton, *The Navaho,* rev. ed. (Cambridge, Mass.: Harvard University Press, 1974).

38. Johnston, *Analysis of Sources of Information,* 22.

39. Ruth Roessel, ed., *Navajo Stories of the Long Walk Period* (Tsaile, Ariz.: Navajo Community College Press, 1973); Katherine Marie Birmingham Osburn, "The Navajo at the Bosque Redondo: Cooperation, Resistance, and Initiative, 1864–1868," *New Mexico Historical Review* 60 (1985): 399–413; and Doolittle Report, U.S. Senate, *Condition of the Indian Tribes.*

40. Doolittle Report, 316–19.

41. Tiana Bighorse, *Bighorse the Warrior* (Tucson: University of Arizona Press, 1990).

42. Frank McNitt, *The Indian Traders* (Norman: University of Oklahoma Press, 1962); John Adair, *The Navajo and Pueblo Silversmiths* (Norman: University of Oklahoma Press, 1944); and James M. Goodman, *The Navajo Atlas: Environments, Resources, People, and History of the Dine Bikeyah* (Norman: University of Oklahoma Press, 1982).

43. Peter Iverson, *The Navajo Nation* (Albuquerque: University of New Mexico Press, 1981); Laurence C. Kelly, *The Navajo Indians and Federal Indian Policy, 1900–1935* (Tucson: University of Arizona Press, 1968); and Donald L. Parman, *The Navajos and the New Deal* (New Haven, Conn.: Yale University Press, 1976).

44. Besides those sources already mentioned, also see, for example, George A. Hillery, Jr., "Navajos and Eastern Kentuckians: A Comparative Study in the Cultural Consequences of the Demographic Transition," *American Anthropologist* 68 (1966): 52–70; George A. Hillery, Jr., and Frank J. Essene, "Navajo Population: An Analysis of the 1960 Census," *Southwestern Journal of Anthropology* 19 (1963): 297–313; Stephen J. Kunitz and John C. Slocumb, "The Changing Sex Ratio of the Navajo Tribe," *Social Biology* 23 (1976): 33–44; Stephen J. Kunitz, "Navajo and Hopi Fertility, 1971–1972," *Human Biology* 46 (1974): 435–51; and Larry R. Stucki, "The Case Against Population Control: The Probable Creation of the First American Indian State," *Human Organization* 30 (1971): 393–99.

45. Johansson and Preston, "Tribal Demography," 1–33; Stephen J. Kunitz, *Disease Change and the Role of Medicine: The Navajo Experience* (Berkeley: University of California Press, 1983), chap. 2; and Stephen J. Kunitz, *Disease and Social Diversity: The European Impact on the Health of Non-Europeans* (New York: Oxford University Press, 1994).

46. Johnston, *Analysis of Sources of Information,* 135. The trading post as a central meeting place for Navajos may have contributed to the spread of epidemic disease. For a graphic description of the horrendous effect of the influenza epidemic on the Navajo Reservation, see Frances Gillmor and Louisa Wade Wetherill, *Traders to the Navajos: The Story of the Wetherills of Kayenta* (Albuquerque: University of New Mexico Press, 1953), 223–29.

47. Abdel R. Omran, "The Epidemiologic Transition: A Theory of the Epidemiology of Population Change," *Milbank Memorial Fund Quarterly* 49 (1971): 509–38.

48. Putney, "Fighting the Scourge"; Gregory Ray Campbell, "The Political Economy of Ill-Health: Changing Northern Cheyenne Health Patterns and Economic Underdevel-

opment, 1878–1930," Ph.D. diss., University of Oklahoma, 1987; Kunitz, *Disease Change;* Broudy and May, "Demographic and Epidemiologic Transition," 1–16; Carr and Lee, "Navajo Tribal Mortality," 279–87; Hackenberg and Gallagher, "Costs of Cultural Change," 211–26; and T. Kue Young, *Health Care and Cultural Change: The Indian Experience in the Central Subarctic* (Toronto: University of Toronto Press, 1988), 48–58.

49. Trafzer, *Death Stalks the Yakama.*

CHAPTER THREE

1. Campbell, "Political Economy of Ill-Health"; and Kenneth Morgan, "Historical Demography of a Navajo Community," in *Methods and Theories of Anthropological Genetics,* ed. M. H. Crawford and P. L. Workman (Albuquerque: University of New Mexico Press, 1973), 263–314.

2. William Brass and Ansley J. Coale, "Methods of Analysis and Estimation," in *The Demography of Tropical Africa,* ed. William Brass et al. (Princeton, N.J.: Princeton University Press, 1968), 88–139; and Shryock and Siegel, *Methods and Materials of Demography,* 499–500; I used a software version of Brass's method, "Mortpak: The United Nations Software Packages for Mortality Measurement" (Population Division, United Nations, 20 Sept. 1986) and selected Coale and Demeny's Model Life Tables-West as the appropriate set of life tables for Indians, whites, and blacks. See Coale and Demeny, *Regional Model Life Tables.*

3. U.S. Bureau of the Census, *Historical Statistics of the United States: Colonial Times to 1970* (Washington, D.C.: GPO, 1975), pt. 1, 55.

4. Shryock and Siegel, *Methods and Materials of Demography,* 499.

5. Johansson and Preston, *Tribal Demography,* 1–33. Johnston also used the Navajos' "fear" of the dead to explain the inadequacy of death registration statistics on the Navajo Reservation, *Analysis of Sources of Information,* 149.

6. Clifford Trafzer examines in more detail the causes of Yakama mortality in this time period in *Death Stalks the Yakama.*

7. For a description of own-children methods, see Lee-Jay Cho, Wilson H. Grabill, and Donald J. Bogue, *Differential Fertility in the United States* (Chicago: Community and Family Study Center, University of Chicago, 1970); and Rindfuss and Sweet, *Postwar Fertility Trends,* 9–31; for discussion of both own-children and children-ever-born measures of fertility, see chap. 17 in Shryock and Siegel, *Methods and Materials of Demography.*

8. Engerman, "Changes in Black Fertility," 126–153; Coale and Zelnik, *New Estimates of Fertility;* and Jenny Bourne Wall, "New Results on the Decline in Household Fertility in the United States from 1750 to 1900," in *Long-Term Factors in American Economic Growth,* ed. Stanley L. Engerman and Robert E. Gallman (Chicago: University of Chicago Press, 1986), 391–437.

9. See, for example, E. A. Wrigley and R. S. Schofield, *The Population History of England, 1541–1871: A Reconstruction* (London: Edward Arnold, 1981); and J. Hajnal, "European Marriage Patterns in Perspective," in *Population in History: Essays in Historical Demography,* ed. D. V. Glass and D. E. C. Eversley (Chicago: Aldine, 1965), 101–143.

10. Schuster, "Yakima Indian Traditionalism"; Donaldson, *Six Nations,* 54; Bernhard J. Stern, "The Letters of Asher Wright to Lewis Henry Morgan," *American Anthropologist* 35 (1933): 138–45; McLoughlin, *Cherokee Renascence,* 332; Frances Densmore,

Chippewa Customs, Bureau of American Ethnology Bulletin 86 (Washington, D.C.: Smithsonian Institution, 1929), 72–73; Gary Witherspoon, *Navajo Kinship and Marriage* (Chicago: University of Chicago Press, 1975), 23–28; and Franc Johnson Newcomb, *Navaho Neighbors* (Norman: University of Oklahoma Press, 1966), 148–60.

11. Walter Dyk, *Son of Old Man Hat: A Navaho Autobiography* (Lincoln: University of Nebraska Press, 1938), 373–78. A similar confusion could have occurred among Cherokee-speaking Cherokees, whose two words for "wife" translated to either "the woman who cooks for me" or "the woman who sleeps with me." See *Cherokee Nation vs. Chucooah Manus* (1888), Flint District Criminal Court Records, vol. 103, Cherokee Nation Papers, microfilm reel no. 38, Oklahoma Historical Society, Oklahoma City.

12. For a description and application of this method, see Steven Ruggles, "The Demography of the Unrelated Individual: 1900–1950," *Demography* 25 (1988): 521–36.

13. Thomas K. Burch, "The Impact of Forms of Families and Sexual Unions and Dissolution of Unions on Fertility," in *Determinants of Fertility in Developing Countries,* ed. Rodolfo A. Bulatao and Ronald D. Lee (New York: Academic Press, 1983), 1: 532–61; Michel Garenne and Etienne Van de Walle, "Polygyny and Fertility Among the Sereer of Senegal," *Population Studies* 43 (1989): 267–83; and Lee L. Bean and Geraldine P. Mineau, "The Polygyny-Fertility Hypothesis: A Re-evaluation," *Population Studies* 40 (1986): 67–81.

14. Kluckhohn and Leighton, *The Navaho,* 100.

15. The 1900 census supplemental Indian form asked whether individuals were living in polygamy. However, the results were erratic. Of Seneca married men, 22 percent have "yes" written in response to the polygamy question, but polygamy was not a Seneca custom. Some enumerators or respondents may not have known what polygamy meant or may have confused it with adultery or number of times married. Since Courts of Indian Offenses on most reservations were brutally punishing polygamists, presumably census respondents would not have readily admitted it to enumerators; Donaldson, *Six Nations of New York,* 54. For more on the government's assimilation programs, see Frederick E. Hoxie, *A Final Promise: The Campaign to Assimilate the Indians: 1880–1920* (Lincoln: University of Nebraska Press, 1984); and William T. Hagan, *Indian Police and Judges* (New Haven, Conn.: Yale University Press, 1966).

16. Louis Henry, "Some Data on Natural Fertility," *Eugenics Quarterly* 8 (1961): 81–91. See also Henry Leridon and Jane Menken, *Natural Fertility: Patterns and Determinants of Natural Fertility, Proceedings of a Seminar on Natural Fertility* (Paris: Ordina Editions, 1977); and John Knodel, "Natural Fertility: Age Patterns, Levels, and Trends," in *Determinants of Fertility in Developing Countries,* ed. Rodolfo A. Bulatao and Ronald D. Lee, 1: 61–102. For a discussion of the many factors leading to low fertility in pretransition societies, see Moni Nag, "How Modernization Can Also Increase Fertility," *Current Anthropology* 21 (1980): 571–87.

17. John C. Ewers, "Contraceptive Charms Among the Plains Indians," *Plains Anthropologist* 15 (1970): 216–18; June Helm, "Female Infanticide, European Diseases, and Population Levels Among the MacKenzie Dene," *American Ethnologist* 7 (1980): 259–85; Ales Hrdlicka, *Physiological and Medical Observations Among the Indians of Southwestern United States and Northern Mexico,* Bureau of American Ethnology Bulletin 34 (Washington, D.C.: Smithsonian Institution, 1908), 163–65; "Laws of the Cherokee Nation, Enacted by the General Council in 1826, 1827, & 1828" (New Echota, C.N.: Isaac Heylin Harris, 1828); Arthur C. Parker, "The Code of Handsome Lake," in

Parker on the Iroquois, ed. William N. Fenton (Syracuse, N.Y.: Syracuse University Press, 1968), 30; and William Engelbrecht, "Factors Maintaining Low Population Density Among the Prehistoric Iroquois," *American Antiquity* 52 (1987): 13–27.

18. William L. Stone, *The Life and Times of Red-Jacket, or Sa-go-ye-wat-ha; Being the Sequel to the History of the Six Nations* (New York: Wiley and Putnam, 1841), 401.

19. Parker, "Code of Handsome Lake," 30; Asher Bliss Journal, Jan. 1833, Bliss Family Papers, New York State Library, Albany, N.Y.

20. M. Hillary's report, ARCIA, 1866, 151. See also Roberto Mario Salmon, "The Disease Complaint at Bosque Redondo (1864–68)," *The Indian Historian* 9 (1976): 2–7.

21. Douglas L. Anderton and Lee L. Bean, "Birth Spacing and Fertility Limitation: A Behavioral Analysis of a Nineteenth Century Frontier Population," *Demography* 22 (1985): 169–83; Lee L. Bean, Geraldine P. Mineau, and Douglas L. Anderton, *Fertility Change on the American Frontier: Adaptation and Innovation* (Berkeley: University of California Press, 1990); John Knodel, "Family Limitation and the Fertility Transition: Evidence from the Age Patterns of Fertility in Europe and Asia," *Population Studies* 31 (1977): 219–49; Knodel, "Natural Fertility"; Knodel, "Starting, Stopping, and Spacing During the Early Stages of Fertility Transition: The Experience of German Village Populations in the 18th and 19th Centuries," *Demography* 24 (1987): 143–62; and Stewart E. Tolnay and Avery M. Guest, "American Family Building Strategies in 1900: Stopping or Spacing," *Demography* 21 (1984): 9–18.

22. Singulate mean age at marriage is described in Shryock and Siegel, *Methods and Materials of Demography,* 167. This method for estimating age at stopping is used in Michael R. Haines, *Fertility and Occupation: Population Patterns in Industrialization* (New York: Academic Press, 1979), 134, 136.

23. M. L. Berman, K. Hanson, and I. L. Hellman, "Effect of Breast-feeding on Post-partum Menstruation, Ovulation, and Pregnancy in Alaskan Eskimos," *American Journal of Obstetrics and Gynecology* 114 (1972): 524–34; and Christopher Tietze, *The Effect of Breast-feeding on the Rate of Conception* (New York: International Population Conference, 1961). Two articles on changing lactation patterns and fertility for North American native people are A. Romaniuk, "Increase in Natural Fertility During the Early Stages of Modernization: Canadian Indians Case Study," *Demography* 18 (1981): 157–72; and Larry Blackwood, "Alaska Native Fertility Trends, 1950–1978," *Demography* 18 (1981), 173–79. These two authors found that Indian fertility levels increased before beginning a long-term decline and credited changing breastfeeding patterns (and the effects of lactation on fecundity) as a major cause of the initial fertility increase. However, it should be noted that their data coincidentally span the baby boom, when similar patterns of fertility occurred among non-native women as well.

24. This method of measuring child-spacing ensures that women who are about to give birth to their second child are included in the population at risk. Thus spacing is measured as the percentage of women (whose first child is three years of age and older) who gave birth to a second child within three years. Only women with all their children-ever-born present in the household were included in the analysis, and so the population is probably a little biased in favor of women whose children are still surviving. See Tolnay and Guest, "American Family Building Strategies," 9–18.

25. U.S. Census Office, *Report on Indians Taxed and not Taxed;* Putney, "Fighting the Scourge"; Ales Hrdlicka, *Tuberculosis Among Certain Indian Tribes of the United States,* Smithsonian Institution, Bureau of American Ethnology Bulletin 42 (Washington, D.C.: GPO, 1909).

26. See Joseph A. McFalls, Jr., and Marguerite Harvey McFalls, *Disease and Fertility* (Orlando, Fla.: Academic Press, 1984); and Linton M. Snaith and Tom Barns, "Fertility in Pelvic Tuberculosis: A Report on the Present Position," *The Lancet* 7 (1962): 712–16.

27. U.S. Census Office, *Report on Indians Taxed and Not Taxed,* 603–616.

28. M. Hillary's report, ARCIA, 1866, 150.

29. A three-day cure of a venereal disease, which took place in a sweat lodge, is described in Dyk, *Son of Old Man Hat,* 82–96.

30. McFalls and McFalls, *Disease and Fertility,* 347.

31. Hrdlicka, *Tuberculosis,* 5–6; U.S. Senate, *Tuberculosis Among the North American Indians: Report of a Committee of the National Tuberculosis Association, 28 October 1921,* 67th Cong., 4th sess. (Washington, D.C.: GPO, 1923), 2; and Gregory R. Campbell, "Changing Patterns of Health and Effective Fertility Among the Northern Cheyenne of Montana, 1886–1903," *The American Indian Quarterly* 15 (1991): 339–58.

32. Hrdlicka, *Tuberculosis,* 5–6; Donaldson, *Six Nations of New York,* 7; U.S. Senate, *Tuberculosis,* 15; and Hrdlicka, *Physiological and Medical Observations,* 212.

CHAPTER FOUR

1. Frank W. Notestein, "Population: The Long View," in *Food for the World,* ed. T. W. Schultz (Chicago: University of Chicago Press, 1945), 36–57.

2. Gary Becker, "An Economic Analysis of Fertility," in *Demographic and Economic Change in Developed Countries,* ed. National Bureau of Economic Research (Princeton: Princeton University Press, 1960), 209–40; and Judith Blake, "Are Babies Consumer Durables? A Critique of the Economic Theory of Reproduction," *Population Studies* 22 (1968): 5–25.

3. Richard A. Easterlin, George Alter, and Gretchen A. Condran, "Farms and Farm Families in Old and New Areas: The Northern States in 1860," in *Family and Population in Nineteenth-Century America,* ed. Tamara K. Hareven and Maris A. Vinovskis (Princeton: Princeton University Press, 1978), 22–84; Richard A. Easterlin, "Population Change and Farm Settlement in the Northern United States," *Journal of Economic History* 36 (1976): 45–75; Richard A. Easterlin, "An Economic Framework for Fertility Analysis," *Studies in Family Planning* 6 (1975): 54–63; and Richard A. Easterlin, "Factors in the Decline of Farm Family Fertility in the United States: Some Preliminary Research Results," *Journal of American History* 63 (1976): 600–614. Also see Avery M. Guest and Stewart E. Tolnay, "Children's Roles and Fertility: Late Nineteenth-Century United States," *Social Science History* 7 (1983): 355–80; Yasukichi Yasuba, *Birth Rates of the White Population in the United States, 1800–1860* (Baltimore, Md.: Johns Hopkins University Press, 1961); and Lee A. Craig, *To Sow One Acre More: Childbearing and Farm Productivity in the Antebellum North* (Baltimore, Md.: Johns Hopkins University Press, 1993); Lee L. Bean, Geraldine P. Mineau, and Douglas L. Anderton argue that cultural diffusion was also a factor in frontier fertility in *Fertility Change.*

4. Leibhardt, "Allotment Policy,"; Debo, *And Still the Waters Run;* and Meyer, *White Earth Tragedy.*

5. John C. Caldwell, *Theory of Fertility Decline* (New York: Academic Press, 1982).

6. See Grant Foreman, *Sequoyah* (Norman: University of Oklahoma Press, 1938); and George E. Foster, *Se-Quo-Yah: The American Cadmus and Modern Moses* (Philadelphia: Indian Rights Association, 1885).

7. Devon A. Mihesuah, *Cultivating the Rosebuds: The Education of Women at the Cherokee Female Seminary, 1851–1909* (Urbana: University of Illinois Press, 1993).

8. Johannes Fabian, *Time and the Other: How Anthropology Makes Its Object* (New York: Columbia University Press, 1983). For critiques of the generalizing effects of demographic theories, see Susan Greenhalgh, ed., *Situating Fertility: Anthropology and Demographic Inquiry* (New York: Cambridge University Press, 1995); Susan Greenhalgh, "The Social Construction of Population Science: An Intellectual, Institutional, and Political History of Twentieth-Century Demography," *Comparative Studies in Society and History* 38 (1996): 26–66; and Kunitz, *Disease and Social Diversity*, 4–6.

9. Yet to be studied in any systematic sense, Cherokee intermarriage with traders can be seen in the most common Cherokee surnames. Vann, Ross, and Adair, for example, all date back to particular eighteenth-century Cherokee traders. Seneca incorporation of non-Senecas was achieved primarily through adoption of captives taken in war. Among the most common surnames among the Senecas are Jemison and Jimerson, all variations dating back to a particular woman captive. See James Everett Seaver, *Narrative of the Life of Mrs. Mary Jemison: White Woman of the Genessee*, 20th ed., revised by Charles Delamater Vail (New York: American Scenic and Historic Preservation Society, 1918).

10. Seneca Nation Constitution. In National Archives, *Correspondence of the Office of Indian Affairs (Central Office) and Related Records. Letters Received, 1824–1881,* M234, reel 573.

11. Cherokee Nation intermarriage permits were recorded in court records, kept by each district's court clerk, and preserved in the Cherokee Nation Collection, Oklahoma Historical Society, Oklahoma City (on microfilm).

12. Jacqueline Peterson, "Many Roads to Red River: Metis Genesis in the Great Lakes Region, 1680–1815," in *The New Peoples: Being and Becoming Metis in North America,* ed. Jacqueline Peterson and Jennifer S. H. Brown (Lincoln: University of Nebraska Press, 1985), 37–71; Jennifer Brown, "A Demographic Transition in the Fur Trade Country: Family Sizes and Fertility of Company Officers and Country Wives, ca. 1759–1850," *The Western Canadian Journal of Anthropology* 6 (1976): 61–71; and U.S. Bureau of the Census, *Indian Population of the United States and Alaska* (Washington, D.C.: GPO, 1915), 157–60; analysis of 1900 and 1910 census data for the Creeks and White Earth Ojibways also shows that intermarriage with whites increased Indian fertility and lowered Indian mortality. Nancy Shoemaker, "Demographic Indicators of American Indian Family Life in the Reservation Era," paper presented at the annual meeting of the Organization of American Historians, Washington, D.C., March 1990.

13. Nag, "Modernization," 571–87.

14. Hrdlicka, *Tuberculosis,* 1–7.

15. New York State Assembly, *Report of the Special Committee to Investigate the Indian Problem of the State of New York,* Document no. 51 (1889), 952, 1189.

16. Annual Message of Chief Charles Thompson, 7 November 1876, in Cherokee Collection, Frank Phillips Collection, University of Oklahoma, Norman, quoted in Morris L. Wardell, *A Political History of the Cherokee Nation, 1838–1907.* Also see McLoughlin, *After the Trail of Tears.*

17. See, for example, Peter MacDonald with Ted Schwarz, *The Last Warrior: Peter MacDonald and the Navajo Nation* (New York: Orion Books, 1993), 2, 29. Louise Lamphere, *To Run After Them: Cultural and Social Bases of Cooperation in a Navajo Community* (Tucson: University of Arizona Press, 1977), discusses how sharing is nego-

tiated within contemporary Navajo families. For witchcraft as social control, see Clyde Kluckhohn, *Navaho Witchcraft* (Boston: Beacon Press, 1944).

18. Dyk, *Son of Old Man Hat*, 77–78, 192. Peter MacDonald, in his autobiography, *The Last Warrior*, leaves out the children but makes nearly an identical remark: "Sheep were like money in the bank; the more you had, the better your life, your future, and your family's future" (37).

19. See Frank Lorimer, *Culture and Human Fertility* (Paris: UNESCO, 1954); Kingsley Davis, "Institutional Patterns Favoring High Fertility in Underdeveloped Areas," *Eugenics Quarterly* 2 (1955): 33–39; and Caldwell, *Fertility Decline;* also see the discussion of this literature and relevant research in Burch, "The Impact of Forms of Families and Sexual Unions and Dissolution of Unions on Fertility"; and Thomas K. Burch and Murray Gendell, "Extended Family Structure and Fertility: Some Conceptual and Methodological Issues," *Journal of Marriage and the Family* 32 (1970): 227–36.

20. See, for example, Shireen J. Jejeebhoy, "Household Type and Family Size in Maharashtra, 1970," *Social Biology* 31 (1984): 91–100; Moni Nag, "Family Type and Fertility," *Proceedings of the World Population Conference, 1965* (New York: United Nations, 1965), 2:160–63; and Kanti Pakrasi and Chittaranjan Malaker, "The Relationship Between Family Type and Fertility," *Milbank Memorial Fund Quarterly* 45 (1967): 451–60; also see the review of this research in Burch and Gendell, "Extended Family Structure."

21. Field Matron Emily Miller's report, ARCIA, 1892, 510; also see Helen Schuster's discussion of extended-family households among contemporary Yakamas in "Yakima Indian Traditionalism."

22. Lewis Henry Morgan, *League of the Iroquois* (Secaucus, N.J.: Citadel Press, 1962); Lewis Henry Morgan, *Houses and House-Life of the American Aborigines*, vol. 4 of *Contributions to North American Ethnology* (Washington, D.C.: GPO, 1881); Wallace, *Death and Rebirth;* and Nancy Shoemaker, "From Longhouse to Loghouse: Household Structure Among the Senecas in 1900," *American Indian Quarterly* 15 (1991): 329–38.

23. Kluckhohn and Leighton, *The Navaho*, 109–11; and Witherspoon, *Navajo Kinship and Marriage*, 100–110; Lamphere, *To Run After Them*, 5, 69–105.

CHAPTER FIVE

1. All these issues are also discussed, in considerably more detail, in C. Matthew Snipp's analysis of the 1980 census, *American Indians*.

2. Prucha, *The Great Father;* and Meriam, *The Problem of Indian Administration*.

3. Alison R. Bernstein, *American Indians and World War II: Toward a New Era in Indian Affairs* (Norman: University of Oklahoma Press, 1991); and Nancy Shoemaker, "Urban Indians and Ethnic Choices: American Indian Organizations in Minneapolis, 1920–1950," *Western Historical Quarterly* 19 (1988): 431–47.

4. The 100,000 figure comes from Alan L. Sorkin, "Some Aspects of American Indian Migration," *Social Forces* 48 (1969): 244. For more on relocation, see Larry W. Burt, *Tribalism in Crisis: Federal Indian Policy, 1953–1961* (Albuquerque: University of New Mexico Press, 1982); Lawrence Clinton, Bruce A. Chadwick, and Howard M. Bahr, "Urban Relocation Reconsidered: Antecedents of Employment Among Indian Males," *Rural Sociology* 40 (1975): 117–33; Donald L. Fixico, *Termination and Relocation: Fed-*

eral Indian Policy, 1945–1960 (Albuquerque: University of New Mexico Press, 1986); James H. Gundlach, P. Nelson Reid, and Alden E. Roberts, "Migration, Labor Mobility, and Relocation Assistance: The Case of the American Indian," *Social Service Review* 51 (1977): 464–73; James H. Gundlach and Alden E. Roberts, "Native American Indian Migration and Relocation: Success or Failure," *Pacific Sociological Review* 21 (1978): 117–28; Elaine M. Neils, *Reservation to City: Indian Migration and Federal Relocation,* University of Chicago Department of Geography Research Papers, no. 131 (Chicago: University of Chicago Department of Geography, 1971); Kenneth R. Philp, "Stride Toward Freedom: The Relocation of Indians to Cities, 1952–1960," *Western Historical Quarterly* 16 (1985): 175–90; and Gary D. Sandefur, "American Indian Migration and Economic Opportunities," *International Migration Review* 20 (1986): 55–68. For more on urban Indian migration in general, see Calvin L. Beale, "Migration Patterns of Minorities in the United States," *American Journal of Agricultural Economics* 55 (1973): 938–46; and Russell Thornton, Gary D. Sandefur, and Harold G. Grasmick, *The Urbanization of American Indians: A Critical Bibliography* (Bloomington: Indiana University Press, 1982).

5. U.S. Bureau of the Census, *Sixteenth Census of the United States: 1940. Characteristics of the Nonwhite Population by Race* (Washington, D.C.: GPO, 1943), 6; and U.S. Bureau of the Census, *1980 Census of Population,* vol. I, ch. C, *General Social and Economic Characteristics,* pt. 1, United States Summary (Washington, D.C.: GPO, 1983), 385–89.

6. See League of Women Voters of Minnesota, *The Indian in Minnesota: A Report to Governor Luther W. Youngdahl of Minnesota by the Governor's Interracial Commission* (St. Paul, Minn., 1947), 37. For more on the problems researchers in the 1920s encountered when trying to identify Indians living in cities, see Meriam, *Problem of Indian Administration,* chap. 12.

7. Joane Nagel, "American Indian Ethnic Renewal: Politics and the Resurgence of Identity," *American Sociological Review* 60 (1995): 952.

8. The Census Bureau also refined its classification criteria for urban and rural. The 1940 census defined "urban" as incorporated places with 2,500 or more people; the 1950 census dropped "incorporated" to include unincorporated "urban fringe" places in the urban category. According to the 1940 definition, 59 percent of the 1950 U.S. population was urban, while the 1950 definition increased the percent urban to 64 percent. See U.S. Census Bureau, *Historical Statistics of the United States: Colonial Times to 1970,* 12–13.

9. For more on government boarding schools and Indian experiences at these schools, see K. Tsianina Lomawaima, *They Called It Prairie Light: The Story of Chilocco Indian School* (Lincoln: University of Nebraska Press, 1994); Donal F. Lindsey, *Indians at Hampton Institute, 1877–1923* (Urbana: University of Illinois Press, 1995); and Robert A. Trennert, *The Phoenix Indian School: Forced Assimilation in Arizona, 1891–1935* (Norman: University of Oklahoma Press, 1988). For more on developments in Indian education once boarding schools were on the wane, see Margaret Szasz, *Education and the American Indian: The Road to Self-Determination, 1928–1973* (Albuquerque: University of New Mexico Press, 1974).

10. See the personal reminiscences of Wilma Pearl Mankiller in *Mankiller: A Chief and Her People* (New York: St. Martin's Press, 1993) and in the foreward to Ignatia Broker, *Night Flying Woman: An Ojibway Narrative* (St. Paul: Minnesota Historical Society Press, 1983).

11. The industrial focus of boarding schools is a major theme in Trennert's *Phoenix Indian School* and Lindsey's *Indians at Hampton Institute.*

12. Meriam, *Problem of Indian Administration,* 448.

13. Ibid., 4–7, 460.

14. A more detailed discussion of the questions asked can be found in the codebook: U.S. Bureau of the Census, *Census of Population, 1940 [United States]: Public Use Microdata Sample* (Ann Arbor, Mich.: Inter-University Consortium for Political and Social Research, 1984), 6.18–6.20.

15. Donald L. Parman, "The Indian and the Civilian Conservation Corps," *Pacific Historical Quarterly* 40 (1971): 39–56; Patricia K. Ourada, "Indians in the Work Force," *Journal of the West* 25 (1986): 52–58; and Cardell K. Jacobsen, "Internal Colonialism and Native Americans: Indian Labor in the United States from 1871 to World War II," *Social Science Quarterly* 65 (1984): 158–71.

16. Gary D. Sandefur and Wilbur J. Scott, "Minority Group Status and the Wages of Indian and Black Males," *Social Science Research* 12 (1983): 44–68.

17. Snipp, *American Indians,* 254, 264.

18. The definition of poverty used in the 1980 *Public Use Microdata Sample* incorporates an index of income adjusted for the number of people in the household, number of children under eighteen, and the age of household head ("householder"). See U.S. Bureau of the Census, *Census of Population and Housing, 1980: Public Use Microdata Samples, Technical Documentation* (Washington, D.C.: GPO, 1983), k–33 to k–36.

19. See Snipp, *American Indians,* 256–58, 246, for a more detailed discussion of the causes of these improvements.

20. These findings differ from those in Sandefur and Sakamoto, "American Indian Household Structure and Income," 71–80, who found that Indian households in 1980 were more likely than white or black households to be headed by a married couple. A quirk in their data collection process was bound to lead them to that mistaken conclusion. They extracted a sample of Indians from the 1980 *Public Use Microdata Sample* using the criteria of (1) if the head of the household was racially identified as Indian, or (2) if the spouse of the head was Indian. Because of the high levels of intermarriage among Indians, married Indians had an extra opportunity to be included in the sample and were therefore overrepresented compared to other racial groups (most blacks are married to blacks, and most whites are married to whites).

21. See Mary Jo Banes, "Household Composition and Poverty," in *Fighting Poverty: What Works and What Doesn't,* ed. Sheldon H. Danziger and Daniel H. Weinberg (Cambridge, Mass.: Harvard University Press, 1986), 209–231; James A. Sweet and Larry L. Bumpass, *American Families and Households* (New York: Russell Sage Foundation, 1987); Irwin Garfinkel and Sara S. McLanahan, *Single Mothers and Their Children: A New American Dilemma* (Washington, D.C.: Urban Institute, 1986); Sara McLanahan and Karen Booth, "Mother-Only Families: Problems, Prospects, and Politics," *Journal of Marriage and the Family* 51 (Aug. 1989): 557–80; and William Julius Wilson and Kathryn M. Neckerman, "Poverty and Family Structure: The Widening Gap between Evidence and Public Policy Issues," *Fighting Poverty,* 232–59.

22. Joseph G. Jorgensen, "Indians and the Metropolis," in *The American Indian in Urban Society,* ed. Jack O. Waddell and O. Michael Watson (Boston: Little, Brown and Co., 1971), 67–113; Joseph G. Jorgensen, *The Sun Dance Religion: Power for the Powerless* (Chicago: University of Chicago Press, 1972), chap. 4; and Martha C. Knack, *Life Is with People: Household Organization of the Contemporary Southern Paiute Indians* (Socorro, N.Mex.: Ballena Press, 1980).

23. Mary Crow Dog with Richard Erdoes, *Lakota Woman* (New York: HarperCollins, 1990), 13. Frank Fools Crow expressed some similar frustrations with the financial burden posed by a responsibility to one's relatives in his autobiography, compiled by Thomas E. Mails, *Fools Crow* (Lincoln: University of Nebraska Press, 1979), 179.

24. Sandefur and McKinnell, "American Indian Intermarriage.".

25. Brian W. Dippie, *The Vanishing American: White Attitudes and U.S. Indian Policy* (Middletown, Conn.: Wesleyan University Press, 1982), 243–69; and U.S. Census Bureau, *Indian Population in the United States and Alaska, 1910,* 159.

26. Ronald R. Rindfuss and James A. Sweet noticed this in their study of the baby boom, *Postwar Fertility Trends and Differentials in the United States,* 123–4, and further discussion appears in Thornton, Sandefur, and Snipp, "A Research Note: American Indian Fertility Patterns: 1910 and 1940 to 1980."

27. Rindfuss and Sweet, *Postwar Fertility Trends,* 149; Frank D. Bean and Charles H. Wood, "Ethnic Variations in the Relationship Between Income and Fertility," *Demography* 11 (1974): 629–40; and Nan E. Johnson and Suewen Lean, "Relative Income, Race, and Fertility," *Population Studies* 39 (1985): 99–112.

28. Frank M. Andrews et al., *Multiple Classification Analysis,* 2d ed. (Ann Arbor: University of Michigan Institute for Social Research, 1973).

29. Pronatalism is a recurrent theme in American Indian Movement activist Mary Crow Dog's *Lakota Woman.*

30. Charles R. England, "A Look at the Indian Health Service Policy of Sterilization, 1972–1976," *Red Ink* 3 (1994): 17–21.

31. See, for example, C. M. Doran, "Attitudes of 30 American Indian Women Towards Birth Control," *HSMHA Health Reports* 87 (1972): 658–63; Stephen J. Kunitz and John C. Slocumb, "The Use of Surgery to Avoid Childbearing Among Navajo and Hopi Indians," *Human Biology* 48 (1976): 9–21; Stephen J. Kunitz and M. Tsianco, "Kinship Dependence and Contraceptive Use in a Sample of Navajo Women," *Human Biology* 53 (1981): 439–52; John C. Slocumb, Stephen J. Kunitz, and C. L. Odoroff, "Complications with Use of IUD and Oral Contraceptives Among Navajo Women," *Public Health Reports* 94 (1979): 243–47; and E. E. Wallach, A. E. Beer, and C.-R. Garcia, "Patient Acceptance of Oral Contraceptives, #1: The American Indian," *American Journal of Obstetrics and Gynecology* 97 (1967): 984–91.

32. Greenhalgh, "Social Construction of Population Science," shows how the discipline of demography has too often been driven by the perspective of government policymakers, whose solution to Third World problems was to reduce the population by disseminating information on contraceptive use and family planning. The same policy perspective guided understandings of population and fertility within the United States as well.

CHAPTER SIX

1. Steven Unger, ed., *The Destruction of American Indian Families* (New York: Association on American Indian Affairs, 1977); American Indian Policy Review Commission, Task Force Four, *Report on Federal, State, and Tribal Jurisdiction* (Washington, D.C.: GPO, 1976), 179; Ray Moisa, "The Indian Child Welfare Act Comes of Age," *News from Native California* 2, no. 4; Bill Donovan, "Lady Discovers her Diné Family, Roots,"

Navajo Times 35, no. 19, 9 May 1996, 1; and Renee S. Flood, *Lost Bird of Wounded Knee: Spirit of the Lakota* (New York: Scribner, 1995).

2. See the five-part series in *Indian Country Today*, 4 Jan. 1996–17 Apr. 1996, p. A1.

3. Orlan J. Svingen, "Jim Crow, Indian Style," *American Indian Quarterly* 11 (1987): 275–86; Kenneth R. Weber, "Demographic Shifts in Eastern Montana Reservation Counties: An Emerging Native American Political Power Base?" *Journal of Ethnic Studies* 16 (1989): 101–16; and Stephen Cornell, *The Return of the Native: American Indian Political Resurgence* (New York: Oxford University Press, 1988).

APPENDIX

1. For a comparison of BIA enrollment censuses and the U.S. census, see Shoemaker, "Census as Civilizer."

2. These are at the New York State Archives, Albany, New York.

3. Hurtado, *Indian Survival on the California Frontier*.

4. Apparently the government collected these data but never synthesized the data into publishable findings. The manuscript forms are in Record Group 29, National Archives, Washington, D.C., and are available on microfilm.

5. Stephen N. Graham, "1900 Public Use Sample: User's Handbook" (draft version) (Seattle: Center for Studies in Demography and Ecology, University of Washington, 1980), 20.

6. For more on this issue, see my article "Census as Civilizer."

7. Shryock and Siegel, *Methods and Materials of Demography*, 167.

8. For more on the U.S. public use samples, see Steven Ruggles, "Comparability of the Public Use Files of the U.S. Census of Population, 1880–1980," *Social Science History* 51 (1991): 123–58. Also see the codebooks: Graham, "1900 Public Use Sample"; Michael A. Strong et al., *User's Guide: Public Use Sample: 1910 United States Census of Population* (Philadelphia: Population Studies Center, University of Pennsylvania, January 1989); U.S. Bureau of the Census, *Census of Population, 1940 [United States]: Public Use Microdata Sample;* U.S. Bureau of the Census, *United States Census Data for 1960* (Ann Arbor, Mich.: ICPSR, 1973); U.S. Bureau of the Census, *Public Use Samples of Basic Records from the 1970 Census: Description and Technical Documentation* (Washington, D.C., 1972); and U.S. Bureau of the Census, *Census of Population and Housing, 1980: Public Use Microdata Samples: Technical Documentation.*

BIBLIOGRAPHY

ARCIA *Annual Report of the Commissioner of Indian Affairs.* Washington D.C.: GPO, 1850–1907.

Aberle, S. B. D. "Child Mortality Among Pueblo Indians." *American Journal of Physical Anthropology* 16 (1932): 339–49.

———. "Maternal Mortality Among the Pueblos." *American Journal of Physical Anthropology* 18 (1934): 431–35.

Abler, Thomas. "Factional Dispute and Party Conflict in the Political System of the Seneca Nation, 1845–1895: An Ethnohistorical Analysis." Ph.D. diss., University of Toronto, 1969.

Abler, Thomas S. "The Kansas Connection: The Seneca Nation and the Iroquois Confederacy Council." In *Extending the Rafters: Interdisciplinary Approaches to Iroquoian Studies,* ed. Michael K. Foster, Jack Campisi, and Marianne Mithun, 81–93. Albany: State University of New York Press, 1984.

Adair, James. *The History of the American Indians.* 1775. Reprint, New York: Johnson Reprints, 1968.

Adair, John. *The Navajo and Pueblo Silversmiths.* Norman: University of Oklahoma Press, 1944.

American Indian Policy Review Commission, Task Force Four. *Report on Federal, State, and Tribal Jurisdiction.* Washington, D.C.: GPO, 1976.

Anastasio, Angelo. "The Southern Plateau: An Ecological Analysis of Intergroup Relations." *Northwest Anthropological Research Notes* 6 (1972): 109–229.

Anderton, Douglas L., and Lee L. Bean. "Birth Spacing and Fertility Limitation: A Behavioral Analysis of a Nineteenth Century Frontier Population." *Demography* 22 (1985): 169–83.

Andrade, Ron. "Are Tribes Too Exclusive?" *American Indian Journal* 6 (1980): 12–13.

Andrews, Frank M. et al. *Multiple Classification Analysis.* 2d ed. Ann Arbor: University of Michigan, 1973.

Bachman, Ronet. *Death and Violence on the Reservation: Homicide, Family Violence, and Suicide in American Indian Populations.* New York: Auburn House, 1992.

Banes, Mary Jo. "Household Composition and Poverty." In *Fighting Poverty: What Works and What Doesn't,* ed. Sheldon H. Danziger and Daniel H. Weinberg, 209–31. Cambridge, Mass.: Harvard University Press, 1986.

Barnett, H. G. *The Yakima Indians in 1942.* Eugene, Oreg.: Department of Anthropology, University of Oregon, 1969.

Barrow, Mark V., Jerry D. Niswander, and Robert Fortuine. *Health and Disease of American Indians North of Mexico: A Bibliography, 1800–1969.* Gainesville: University of Florida Press, 1972.

Barrows, Robert G. "Instructions of Enumerators for Completing the 1900 Census Population Schedule." *Historical Methods Newsletter* 9 (1976): 201–12.

Beale, Calvin L. "Migration Patterns of Minorities in the United States." *American Journal of Agricultural Economics* 55 (1973): 938–46.

Bean, Frank D., and Charles H. Wood. "Ethnic Variations in the Relationship Between Income and Fertility." *Demography* 11 (1974): 629–40.

Bean, Lee L., and Geraldine P. Mineau. "The Polygyny-Fertility Hypothesis: A Reevaluation." *Population Studies* 40 (1986): 67–81.

Bean, Lee L., Geraldine P. Mineau, and Douglas L. Anderton. *Fertility Change on the American Frontier: Adaptation and Innovation.* Berkeley: University of California Press, 1990.

Becker, Gary. "An Economic Analysis of Fertility." In *Demographic and Economic Change in Developed Countries,* ed. National Bureau of Economic Research, 209–40. Princeton, N.J.: Princeton University Press, 1960.

Benavides, Alonso de. *The Memorial of Fray Alonso de Benavides, 1630.* Albuquerque, N.Mex.: Horn and Wallace, 1965.

Benson, Todd. "Race, Health, and Power: The Federal Government and American Indian Health, 1909–1955." Ph.D. diss., Stanford University, 1994.

Berman, M. L., K. Hanson, and I. L. Hellman. "Effect of Breast-Feeding on Post-Partum Menstruation, Ovulation, and Pregnancy in Alaskan Eskimos." *American Journal of Obstetrics and Gynecology* 114 (1972): 524–34.

Bernstein, Alison R. *American Indians and World War II: Toward a New Era in Indian Affairs.* Norman: University of Oklahoma Press, 1991.

Bighorse, Tiana. *Bighorse the Warrior.* Tucson: University of Arizona Press, 1990.

Blackwood, Larry. "Alaska Native Fertility Trends, 1950–1978." *Demography* 18 (1981): 173–79.

Blake, Judith. "Are Babies Consumer Durables? A Critique of the Economic Theory of Reproductive Motivation." *Population Studies* 22 (Mar. 1968): 5–25.

Blasingham, Emily J. "The Depopulation of the Illinois Indians." Part 2. *Ethnohistory* 3 (1956): 361–412.

Bliss Family. Papers. New York State Library, Albany, N.Y.

Blu, Karen I. *The Lumbee Problem: The Making of an American Indian People.* Cambridge: Cambridge University Press, 1980.

Boyd, Robert Thomas. "The Introduction of Infectious Diseases Among the Indians of the Pacific Northwest, 1774–1874." Ph.D. diss., University of Washington, 1985.

Brass, William, and Coale, Ansley J. "Methods of Analysis and Estimation." In *The Demography of Tropical Africa,* ed. William Brass et al., 88–139. Princeton, N.J.: Princeton University Press, 1968.

Brill, Charles. *Red Lake Nation: Portraits of Ojibway Life*. Minneapolis: University of Minnesota Press, 1992.

Broker, Ignatia. *Night Flying Woman: An Ojibway Narrative*. St. Paul: Minnesota Historical Society Press, 1983.

Broudy, David W., and Philip A. May. "Demographic and Epidemiologic Transition Among the Navajo Indians." *Social Biology* 30 (1983): 1–16.

Brown, Jennifer. "A Demographic Transition in the Fur Trade Country: Family Sizes and Fertility of Company Officers and Country Wives, ca. 1759–1850." *The Western Canadian Journal of Anthropology* 6 (1976): 61–71.

Bulatao, Rodolfo A., and Ronald D. Lee, eds. *Determinants of Fertility in Developing Countries*. 2 vols. New York: Academic Press, 1983.

Burch, Thomas K. "The Impact of Forms of Families and Sexual Unions and Dissolution of Unions on Fertility." In *Determinants of Fertility in Developing Countries*, ed. Rodolfo A. Bulatao and Ronald D. Lee, 2:532–61.

Burch, Thomas K., and Murray Gendell. "Extended Family Structure and Fertility: Some Conceptual and Methodological Issues." *Journal of Marriage and the Family* 32 (May 1970): 227–36.

Burt, Larry W. *Tribalism in Crisis: Federal Indian Policy, 1953–1961*. Albuquerque: University of New Mexico Press, 1982.

Caldwell, John C. *Theory of Fertility Decline*. New York: Academic Press, 1982.

Campbell, Gregory R. "Changing Patterns of Health and Effective Fertility Among the Northern Cheyenne of Montana, 1886–1903." *The American Indian Quarterly* 15 (1991): 339–58.

Campbell, Gregory Ray. "The Political Economy of Ill-Health: Changing Northern Cheyenne Health Patterns and Economic Underdevelopment, 1878–1930." Ph.D. diss., University of Oklahoma, 1987.

Carr, Barbara A., and Eun Sul Lee. "Navajo Tribal Mortality: A Life Table Analysis of the Leading Causes of Death." *Social Biology* 25 (1978): 279–87.

Cherokee Intermarriage Cases. 202 US 76 (1906).

Cherokee Nation Court Records. In the Cherokee Nation Papers, Oklahoma Historical Society, Oklahoma City (on microfilm).

Cho, Lee-Jay, Wilson H. Grabill, and Donald J. Bogue. *Differential Fertility in the United States*. Chicago: Community and Family Study Center, University of Chicago, 1970.

Clinton, Lawrence, Bruce A. Chadwick, and Howard M. Bahr. "Urban Relocation Reconsidered: Antecedents of Employment Among Indian Males." *Rural Sociology* 40 (1975): 117–33.

Coale, Ansley J., and Paul Demeny, with Barbara Vaughan. *Regional Model Life Tables and Stable Populations*. 2d ed. New York: Academic Press, 1983.

Coale, Ansley J., and Zelnik, Melvin. *New Estimates of Fertility and Population in the United States*. Princeton, N.J.: Princeton University Press, 1963.

Cook, Sherburne F. "Interracial Warfare and Population Decline Among the New England Indians." *Ethnohistory* 20 (1973): 1–24.

Cook, Sherburne F., and Borah, Woodrow. *Essays in Population History*. 3 vols. Berkeley: University of California Press, 1971, 1974, 1979.

Cornell, Stephen. *The Return of the Native: American Indian Political Resurgence*. New York: Oxford University Press, 1988.

Coues, Elliott, ed. *The History of the Lewis and Clark Expedition*. Vol. 3. Reprint, New York: Dover, n.d.

Craig, Lee A. *To Sow One Acre More: Childbearing and Farm Productivity in the Antebellum North.* Baltimore, Md.: Johns Hopkins University Press, 1993.

Crosby, Alfred W., Jr. *The Columbian Exchange: Biological and Cultural Consequences of 1492.* Westport, Conn.: Greenwood Press, 1972.

Crow Dog, Mary, with Richard Erdoes. *Lakota Woman.* New York: HarperCollins, 1990.

Daniels, John D. "The Indian Population of North America in 1492." *William and Mary Quarterly* 49 (1992): 298–320.

Daugherty, Richard D. *The Yakima People.* Phoenix, Ariz.: Indian Tribal Series, 1973.

Davis, Kingsley. "Institutional Patterns Favoring High Fertility in Underdeveloped Areas." *Eugenics Quarterly* 2 (1955): 33–39.

Debo, Angie. *And Still the Waters Run: The Betrayal of the Five Civilized Tribes.* Princeton: Princeton University Press, 1940.

———. *The Five Civilized Tribes of Oklahoma: Report on Social and Economic Conditions.* Philadelphia: Indian Rights Association, 1951.

Demos, John. *The Unredeemed Captive: A Family Story from Early America.* New York: Alfred A. Knopf, 1994.

Denevan, William M., ed. *The Native Population of the Americas in 1492.* Madison: University of Wisconsin Press, 1976.

Densmore, Frances. *Chippewa Customs.* Smithsonian Institution, Bureau of American Ethnology Bulletin 86. Washington, D.C., 1929.

Desmond, Gerald R. *Gambling Among the Yakima.* Catholic University of America Anthropological Series, no. 14. Washington, D.C., 1952.

Dippie, Brian W. *The Vanishing American: White Attitudes and U.S. Indian Policy.* Middletown, Conn.: Wesleyan University Press, 1982.

Dobyns, Henry F. "Estimating Aboriginal American Population: An Appraisal of Techniques with a New Hemispheric Estimate." *Current Anthropology* 7 (1966): 395–416.

———. *Native American Historical Demography: A Critical Bibliography.* Bloomington: Indiana University Press, 1976.

———. *Their Number Become Thinned: Native American Population Dynamics in Eastern North America.* Knoxville: University of Tennessee Press, 1983.

Dobyns, Henry, Dean Snow, and Kim Lanphear, and David Henige. "Commentary on Native American Demography." *Ethnohistory* 36 (1989): 285–307.

Donaldson, Thomas. *The Six Nations of New York. Extra Census Bulletin: Indians.* Washington, D.C.: U.S. Census Printing Office, 1892.

Donovan, Bill. "Lady Discovers Her Diné Family, Roots." *Navajo Times* 35 (19) (9 May 1996): 1.

Doolittle Report. See U.S. Senate, "Report of the Joint Special Committee on the Condition of the Indian Tribes."

Doran, C. M. "Attitudes of Thirty American Indian Women Towards Birth Control." *HSMHA Health Reports* 87 (1972): 658–63.

Driver, Harold E. *Indians of North America.* 2d ed. Chicago: University of Chicago Press, 1969.

———. "On the Population Nadir of Indians in the United States." *Current Anthropology* 9 (1968): 330.

Dyk, Walter. *Son of Old Man Hat: A Navaho Autobiography.* Lincoln: University of Nebraska Press, 1938.

Easterlin, Richard A. "An Economic Framework for Fertility Analysis." *Studies in Family Planning* 6 (1975): 54–63.

——. "Factors in the Decline of Farm Family Fertility in the United States: Some Preliminary Research Results." *Journal of American History* 63 (1976): 600–614.

——. "Population Change and Farm Settlement in the Northern United States." *Journal of Economic History* 36 (1976): 45–75.

Easterlin, Richard A., George Alter, and Gretchen A. Condran. "Farms and Farm Families in Old and New Areas: The Northern States in 1860." In *Family and Population in Nineteenth-Century America,* ed. Tamara K. Hareven and Maris A. Vinovskis, 22–84. Princeton, N.J.: Princeton University Press, 1978.

Ebbott, Elizabeth, for the League of Women Voters of Minnesota. *Indians in Minnesota.* 4th ed., rev. Ed. Judith Rosenblatt. Minneapolis: University of Minnesota Press, 1985.

Engelbrecht, William. "Factors Maintaining Low Population Density Among the Prehistoric New York Iroquois." *American Antiquity* 52 (1987): 13–27.

England, Charles R. "A Look at the Indian Health Service Policy of Sterilization, 1972–1976." *Red Ink* 3 (1994): 17–21.

Engerman, Stanley L. "Changes in Black Fertility, 1880–1940." In *Family and Population in Nineteenth-Century America,* ed. Tamara K. Hareven and Maris A. Vinovskis, 126–53. Princeton, N.J.: Princeton University Press, 1978.

Eschbach, Karl. "Changing Identification Among American Indians and Alaska Natives." *Demography* 30 (1993): 635–51.

——. "The Enduring and Vanishing American Indian: American Indian Population Growth and Intermarriage in 1900." *Ethnic and Racial Studies* 18 (1995): 89–108.

Everett, Dianna. *The Texas Cherokees: A People Between Two Fires, 1819–1840.* Norman: University of Oklahoma Press, 1990.

Ewers, John C. "Contraceptive Charms Among the Plains Indians." *Plains Anthropologist* 15 (1970): 216–18.

——. "The Influence of Epidemics on the Indian Populations and Cultures of Texas." *Plains Anthropologist* 18 (1973): 104–15.

Fabian, Johannes. *Time and the Other: How Anthropology Makes Its Object.* New York: Columbia University Press, 1983.

Fixico, Donald L. *Termination and Relocation: Federal Indian Policy, 1945–1960.* Albuquerque: University of New Mexico Press, 1986.

Flood, Renee S. *Lost Bird of Wounded Knee: Spirit of the Lakota.* New York: Scribner, 1995.

Foreman, Grant. *Sequoyah.* Norman: University of Oklahoma Press, 1938.

Foster, George E. *Se-Quo-Yah: The American Cadmus and Modern Moses.* Philadelphia: Indian Rights Association, 1885.

Garenne, Michel, and Etienne Van de Walle. "Polygyny and Fertility Among the Sereer of Senegal." *Population Studies* 43 (1989): 267–83.

Garfinkel, Irwin, and Sara S. McLanahan. *Single Mothers and Their Children: A New American Dilemma.* Washington, D.C.: Urban Institute, 1986.

Gillmor, Frances, and Louisa Wade Wetherill. *Traders to the Navajos: The Story of the Wetherills of Kayenta.* Albuquerque: University of New Mexico Press, 1953.

Goodman, James M. *The Navajo Atlas: Environments, Resources, People, and History of the Dine Bikeyah.* Norman: University of Oklahoma Press, 1982.

Grabill, Wilson H., Clyde V. Kiser, and Pascal K. Whelpton. *The Fertility of American Women*. New York: Wiley, 1958.

Graham, Stephen N. "1900 Public Use Sample: User's Handbook. Draft version." Seattle: Center for Studies in Demography and Ecology, University of Washington, 1980.

Graymont, Barbara. *The Iroquois in the American Revolution*. Syracuse, N.Y.: Syracuse University Press, 1972.

Greenbaum, Susan. "What's in a Label? Identity Problems of Southern Indian Tribes." *Journal of Ethnic Studies* 19 (1991): 107–26.

Greenhalgh, Susan. "The Social Construction of Population Science: An Intellectual, Institutional, and Political History of Twentieth-Century Demography." *Comparative Studies in Society and History* 38 (1996): 26–66.

———, ed. *Situating Fertility: Anthropology and Demographic Inquiry*. New York: Cambridge University Press, 1995.

Guest, Avery M., and Stewart E. Tolnay. "Children's Roles and Fertility: Late Nineteenth-Century United States." *Social Science History* 7 (1983): 355–80.

Gundlach, James H., P. Nelson Reid, and Alden E. Roberts. "Migration, Labor Mobility, and Relocation Assistance: The Case of the American Indian." *Social Service Review* 51 (1977): 464–73.

Gundlach, James H., and Alden E. Roberts. "Native American Indian Migration and Relocation: Success or Failure?" *Pacific Sociological Review* 21 (1978): 117–28.

Hackenberg, Robert A., and Mary M. Gallagher. "The Costs of Cultural Change: Accidental Injury and Modernization among the Papago Indians." *Human Organization* 31 (1972): 211–26.

Hagan, William T. "Full Blood, Mixed Blood, Generic, and Ersatz: The Problem of Indian Identity." *Arizona and the West* 27 (1985): 309–26.

———. *Indian Police and Judges*. New Haven, Conn.: Yale University Press, 1966.

Haines, Michael R. *Fertility and Occupation: Population Patterns in Industrialization*. New York: Academic Press, 1979.

Hajnal, J. "European Marriage Patterns in Perspective." In *Population in History: Essays in Historical Demography*, ed. D. V. Glass and D. E. C. Eversley, 101–143. Chicago: Aldine, 1965.

Harris, David. "The 1990 Census Count of American Indians: What Do the Numbers Really Mean?" *Social Science Quarterly* 75 (1994): 580–93.

Hauptman, Laurence M. *The Iroquois and the New Deal*. Syracuse, N.Y.: Syracuse University Press, 1981.

———. *The Iroquois Struggle for Survival: World War II to Red Power*. Syracuse, N.Y.: Syracuse University Press, 1986.

Helm, June. "Female Infanticide, European Diseases, and Population Levels Among the MacKenzie Dene." *American Ethnologist* 7 (1980): 259–85.

Hemming, John. *Amazon Frontier: The Defeat of the Brazilian Indians*. Cambridge, Mass.: Harvard University Press, 1987.

Henige, David. "If Pigs Could Fly: Timucuan Population and Native American Historical Demography." *Journal of Interdisciplinary History* 16 (1986): 701–20.

———. "On the Contact Population of Hispaniola: History as Higher Mathematics." *Hispanic American Historical Review* 58 (1978): 217–37.

Henry, Louis. "Some Data on Natural Fertility." *Eugenics Quarterly* 8 (1961): 81–91.

Hillery, George A., Jr. "Navajos and Eastern Kentuckians: A Comparative Study in the Cultural Consequences of the Demographic Transition." *American Anthropologist* 68 (1966): 52–70.

Hillery, George A., Jr., and Frank J. Essene. "Navajo Population: An Analysis of the 1960 Census." *Southwestern Journal of Anthropology* 19 (1963): 297–313.

Hough, Franklin B. *Census of the State of New York for 1855.* Albany: Charles Van Benthuysen and Sons, 1857.

———. *Census of the State of New York for 1865.* Albany: Charles Van Benthuysen and Sons, 1867.

———. *Census of the State of New York for 1875.* Albany: Charles Van Benthuysen and Sons, 1877.

Howard, Cheryl. *Navajo Tribal Demography, 1983–1986: A Comparative and Historical Perspective.* New York: Garland, 1993.

Howard, R. Palmer. "Cherokee History to 1840: A Medical View." *Oklahoma State Medical Association Journal* 63 (1970): 71–82.

Hoxie, Frederick E. *A Final Promise: The Campaign to Assimilate the Indians: 1880–1920.* Lincoln: University of Nebraska Press, 1984.

Hrdlicka, Ales. *Physiological and Medical Observations Among the Indians of Southwestern United States and Northern Mexico.* Smithsonian Institution, Bureau of American Ethnology Bulletin 34. Washington, D.C., 1908.

———. *Tuberculosis Among Certain Indian Tribes of the United States.* Smithsonian Institution, Bureau of American Ethnology Bulletin 42. Washington, D.C., 1909.

Hudson, Charles. *The Southeastern Indians.* Knoxville: University of Tennessee Press, 1976.

Hunn, Eugene S. *Nch'i-Wána, "The Big River": Mid-Columbia Indians and Their Land.* Seattle: University of Washington Press, 1990.

Hurtado, Albert L. *Indian Survival on the California Frontier.* New Haven, Conn.: Yale University Press, 1988.

Iverson, Peter. *The Navajo Nation.* Albuquerque: University of New Mexico Press, 1981.

Jacobs, Wilbur R. "The Tip of an Iceberg: Pre-Columbian Indian Demography and Some Implications for Revisionism." *William and Mary Quarterly* 31 (1974): 123–32.

Jacobsen, Cardell K. "Internal Colonialism and Native Americans: Indian Labor in the United States from 1871 to World War II." *Social Science Quarterly* 65 (1984): 158–71.

Jaimes, M. Annette. "Federal Indian Identification Policy: A Usurpation of Indigenous Sovereignty in North America." In *Native Americans and Public Policy,* ed. Fremont J. Lyden and Lyman H. Legters, 113–35. Pittsburgh, Penn.: University of Pittsburgh Press, 1992.

Jejeebhoy, Shireen J. "Household Type and Family Size in Maharashtra, 1970." *Social Biology* 31 (1984): 91–100.

Johansson, S. Ryan. "The Demographic History of the Native Peoples of North America: A Selective Bibliography." *Yearbook of Physical Anthropology* 25 (1982): 133–52.

Johansson, S. Ryan, and S. Horrowitz. "Estimating Mortality in Skeletal Populations: The Influence of the Growth Rate on the Interpretation of Levels and Trends During the Transition to Agriculture." *American Journal of Physical Anthropology* 71 (1986): 233–50.

Johansson, S. Ryan, and S. H. Preston. "Tribal Demography: The Hopi and Navaho Populations As Seen Through Manuscripts from the 1900 U.S. Census." *Social Science History* 3 (1978): 1–33.

Johnson, Nan E., and Suewen Lean. "Relative Income, Race, and Fertility." *Population Studies* 39 (1985): 99–112.

Johnston, Denis Foster. *An Analysis of Sources of Information on the Population of the Navaho.* Smithsonian Institution, Bureau of American Ethnology Bulletin 197. Washington, D.C.: GPO, 1966.

Jorgensen, Joseph G. "Indians and the Metropolis." In *The American Indian in Urban Society,* ed Jack O. Waddell and O. Michael Watson, 67–113. Boston: Little, Brown and Co., 1971.

———. *The Sun Dance Religion: Power for the Powerless.* Chicago: University of Chicago Press, 1972.

Kelly, Lawrence C. *The Navajo Indians and Federal Indian Policy, 1900–1935.* Tucson: University of Arizona Press, 1968.

Kennedy, Richard D., and Roger E. Deapen. "Differences Between Oklahoma Indian Infant Mortality and Other Races." *Public Health Reports* 106 (1991): 97–99.

Kenen, Regina, and Charles R. Hammerslough. "Reservation and Non-Reservation American Indian Mortality in 1970 and 1978." *Social Biology* 34 (1987): 26–36.

Kirkland, Samuel. "Census of Six Nations Giving Names of Tribes and Heads of Families. October 20, 1789." Samuel Kirkland Papers, Hamilton College Library, Clinton, N.Y.

Kluckhohn, Clyde. *Navaho Witchcraft.* 1944. Reprint, Boston: Beacon Press, 1967.

Kluckhohn, Clyde, and Leighton, Dorothea. *The Navaho.* Rev. ed. Cambridge, Mass.: Harvard University Press, 1974.

Knack, Martha C. *Life Is With People: Household Organization of the Contemporary Southern Paiute Indians.* Socorro, N.Mex.: Ballena Press, 1980.

Knodel, John. "Family Limitation and the Fertility Transition: Evidence from the Age Patterns of Fertility in Europe and Asia." *Population Studies* 31 (1977): 219–49.

———. "Natural Fertility: Age Patterns, Levels, and Trends." In *Determinants of Fertility in Developing Countries,* ed. Rodolfo A. Bulatao and Ronald D. Lee, 1:61–102. New York: Academic Press, 1982.

———. "Starting, Stopping, and Spacing During the Early Stages of Fertility Transition: The Experience of German Village Populations in the Eighteenth and Nineteenth Centuries." *Demography* 24 (1987): 143–62.

Kroeber, Alfred L. "Cultural and Natural Areas of Native North America." *American Archaeology and Ethnology* 38 (1939).

Kunitz, Stephen J. *Disease and Social Diversity: The European Impact on the Health of Non-Europeans.* New York: Oxford University Press, 1994.

———. *Disease Change and the Role of Medicine: The Navajo Experience.* Berkeley: University of California Press, 1983.

———. "The History and Politics of U.S. Health Care Policy for American Indians and Alaskan Natives." *American Journal of Public Health* 86 (1996): 1464–73.

———. "Navajo and Hopi Fertility, 1971–1972." *Human Biology* 46 (1974): 435–51.

Kunitz, Stephen J., and John C. Slocumb. "The Changing Sex Ratio of the Navajo Tribe." *Social Biology* 23 (1976): 33–44.

———. "The Use of Surgery to Avoid Childbearing Among Navajo and Hopi Indians." *Human Biology* 48 (1976): 9–21.

Kunitz, Stephen J., and M. Tsianco. "Kinship Dependence and Contraceptive Use in a Sample of Navajo Women." *Human Biology* 53 (1981): 439–52.

Lafitau, Joseph François. *Customs of the American Indians Compared with the Customs of Primitive Times.* 2 vols. Ed. and trans. William N. Fenton and Elizabeth L. Moore. Toronto: Champlain Society, 1974, 1977.

Lamphere, Louise. *To Run After Them: Cultural and Social Bases of Cooperation in a Navajo Community.* Tucson: University of Arizona Press, 1977.

Larsen, Clark Spencer, and George R. Miller, eds. *In the Wake of Contact: Biological Responses to Conquest.* New York: Wiley-Liss, 1994.

"Laws of the Cherokee Nation, Enacted by the General Council in 1826, 1827, & 1828." New Echota, C.N.: Isaac Heylin Harris, 1828. In *Laws and Constitution of the American Indian,* Hargrett Collection, on microfilm.

League of Women Voters of Minnesota. *The Indian in Minnesota: A Report to Governor Luther W. Youngdahl of Minnesota by the Governor's Interracial Commission.* St. Paul, Minn., 1947.

Leibhardt, Barbara. "Allotment Policy in an Incongruous Legal System: The Yakima Indian Nation as a Case Study, 1887–1934." *Agricultural History* 65 (1991): 78–103.

Leridon, Henry, and Jane Menken. *Natural Fertility: Patterns and Determinants of Natural Fertility, Proceedings of a Seminar on Natural Fertility.* Paris: Ordina Editions, 1977.

Lindsey, Donal F. *Indians at Hampton Institute, 1877–1923.* Urbana: University of Illinois Press, 1995.

Littlefield, Daniel F. *The Cherokee Freedmen: From Emancipation to American Citizenship.* Westport, Conn.: Greenwood Press, 1978.

Lomawaima, K. Tsianina. *They Called It Prairie Light: The Story of Chilocco Indian School.* Lincoln: University of Nebraska Press, 1994.

Lorimer, Frank. *Culture and Human Fertility.* Paris: UNESCO, 1954.

MacDonald, Peter, with Ted Schwarz. *The Last Warrior: Peter MacDonald and the Navajo Nation.* New York: Orion Books, 1993.

Mails, Thomas E., assisted by Dallas Chief Eagle. *Fools Crow.* Lincoln: University of Nebraska Press, 1979.

Mankiller, Wilma Pearl. *Mankiller: A Chief and Her People.* New York: St. Martin's Press, 1993.

Mason, Karen Oppenheim, Maxine Weinstein, and Barbara Laslett. "The Decline of Fertility in Los Angeles, California, 1880–1900." *Population Studies* 41 (1987): 483–99.

Mason, Philip P., ed. *Schoolcraft's Expedition to Lake Itasca: The Discovery of the Source of the Mississippi.* East Lansing: Michigan State University Press, 1958.

McFalls, Joseph A., Jr., and Marguerite Harvey McFalls. *Disease and Fertility.* Orlando, Fla.: Academic Press, 1984.

McLanahan, Sara, and Karen Booth. "Mother-Only Families: Problems, Prospects, and Politics." *Journal of Marriage and the Family* 51 (1989): 557–80.

McLoughlin, William G. *After the Trail of Tears: The Cherokees' Struggle for Sovereignty, 1839–1880.* Chapel Hill: University of North Carolina Press, 1993.

———. *Cherokee Renascence in the New Republic.* Princeton, N.J.: Princeton University Press, 1986.

McLoughlin, William G., and Walter H. Conser, Jr. "The Cherokees in Transition: A Statistical Analysis of the Federal Cherokee Census of 1835." *Journal of American History* 64 (1977): 678–703.

McNitt, Frank. *The Indian Traders.* Norman: University of Oklahoma Press, 1962.

McWhorter, Lucullus V. *The Crime Against the Yakimas.* North Yakima, Wash.: Republic Print, 1913.

Meister, Cary W. "Methods for Evaluating the Accuracy of Ethnohistorical Demographic Data on North American Indians: A Brief Assessment." *Ethnohistory* 27 (1980): 153–68.

———. "The Misleading Nature of Data in the Bureau of the Census Subject Report on 1970 American Indian Population." *Indian Historian* 11 (1978): 12–19.

Meriam, Lewis, ed. *The Problem of Indian Administration.* Washington, D.C.: Institute for Government Research, 1928.

Merrell, James H. *The Indians' New World: Catawbas and Their Neighbors from European Contact Through the Era of Removal.* Chapel Hill: University of North Carolina Press, 1989.

Meyer, Melissa L. *The White Earth Tragedy: Ethnicity and Dispossession at a Minnesota Anishinaabe Reservation, 1889–1920.* Lincoln: University of Nebraska Press, 1994.

Michelson, Gunther. "Iroquois Population Statistics." *Man in the Northeast* 14 (1977): 3–17.

Mihesuah, Devon A. *Cultivating the Rosebuds: The Education of Women at the Cherokee Female Seminary, 1851–1909.* Urbana: University of Illinois Press, 1993.

Moisa, Ray. "The Indian Child Welfare Act Comes of Age." *News from Native California* 2 (4).

Mooney, James. "The Aboriginal Population of America North of Mexico." In *Smithsonian Miscellaneous Collections,* vol. 80, ed. John R. Swanton, 1–40. Washington, D.C.: Smithsonian Institution, 1928.

———. *Historical Sketch of the Cherokee.* 1900. Reprint, Chicago: Aldine, 1975.

———. "Population." In *Handbook of North American Indians North of Mexico,* ed. Frederick Webb Hodge, 2:287. 2 vols. Smithsonian Institution, Bureau of American Ethnology Bulletin 30. Washington, D.C., 1912.

Morgan, Kenneth. "Historical Demography of a Navajo Community." In *Methods and Theories of Anthropological Genetics,* ed. M. H. Crawford and P. L. Workman, 263–314. Albuquerque: University of New Mexico Press, 1973.

Morgan, Lewis Henry. *Houses and House-Life of the American Aborigines.* Vol. 4 of *Contributions to North American Ethnology.* Washington, D.C.: GPO, 1881.

———. *League of the Iroquois.* Secaucus, N.J.: Citadel Press, 1962.

Nag, Moni. "Family Type and Fertility." In *Proceedings of the World Population Conference, 1965,* 2:160–63. New York: United Nations, 1965.

———. "How Modernization Can Also Increase Fertility." *Current Anthropology* 21 (1980): 571–87.

Nagel, Joane. "American Indian Ethnic Renewal: Politics and the Resurgence of Identity." *American Sociological Review* 60 (1995): 947–65.

———. *American Indian Ethnic Renewal: Red Power and the Resurgence of Identity and Culture.* New York: Oxford University Press, 1996.

National Archives. *The 1900 Federal Population Census.* Microfilm collection, T623.

———. *The 1910 Federal Population Census.* Microfilm collection, T624.

National Vital Statistics Division. "Matched Record Comparison of Birth Certificate and Census Information: United States, 1950." Vital Statistics, Special Reports 47 (12) (19 Mar. 1962): 368.

Neils, Elaine M. *Reservation to City: Indian Migration and Federal Relocation.* University of Chicago Department of Geography Research Papers, no. 131. Chicago: University of Chicago Department of Geography, 1971.

Newcomb, Franc Johnson. *Navaho Neighbors*. Norman: University of Oklahoma Press, 1966.
New York State Assembly. *Report of the Special Committee to Investigate the Indian Problem of the State of New York*. Document no. 51. Albany, N.Y., 1889.
Notestein, Frank W. "Population: The Long View." In *Food For the World*, ed. T. W. Schultz, 36–57. Chicago: University of Chicago Press, 1945.
O'Brien, Sharon. *American Indian Tribal Governments*. Norman: University of Oklahoma Press, 1989.
O'Callaghan, E. B. *The Documentary History of the State of New-York*. 4 vols. Albany: Charles Van Benthuysen, 1851.
Omran, Abdel R. "The Epidemiologic Transition." *The Milbank Memorial Fund Quarterly* 49 (1971): 509–38.
Osburn, Katherine Marie Birmingham. "The Navajo at the Bosque Redondo: Cooperation, Resistance, and Initiative, 1864–1868." *New Mexico Historical Review* 60 (1985): 399–413.
Ourada, Patricia K. "Indians in the Work Force." *Journal of the West* 25 (1986): 52–58.
Paisano, Edna Lee, U.S. Census Bureau. Letter to author, 23 Feb. 1994.
Pakrasi, Kanti, and Chittaranjan Malaker. "The Relationship Between Family Type and Fertility." *Milbank Memorial Fund Quarterly* 45 (1967): 451–60.
Parker, Arthur C. "The Code of Handsome Lake." In *Parker on the Iroquois*, ed. William N. Fenton. Syracuse, N.Y.: Syracuse University Press, 1968.
Parman, Donald L. "The Indian and the Civilian Conservation Corps." *Pacific Historical Quarterly* 40 (1971): 39–56.
——. *The Navajos and the New Deal*. New Haven, Conn.: Yale University Press, 1976.
Passel, Jeffrey S. "Provisional Evaluation of the 1970 Census Count of American Indians." *Demography* 13 (1976): 397–409.
Passel, Jeffrey S., and Patricia A. Berman. "Quality of 1980 Census Data for American Indians." *Social Biology* 33 (1986): 163–82.
Perdue, Theda. *Slavery and the Evolution of Cherokee Society, 1540–1866*. Knoxville: University of Tennessee Press, 1979.
Peterson, Jacqueline. "Many Roads to Red River: Metis Genesis in the Great Lakes Region, 1680–1815." In *The New Peoples: Being and Becoming Metis in North America*, ed. Jacqueline Peterson and Jennifer S. H. Brown, 37–71. Lincoln: University of Nebraska Press, 1985.
Philp, Kenneth R., ed. *Indian Self-Rule: First-Hand Accounts of Indian-White Relations from Roosevelt to Reagan*. Salt Lake City, Utah: Institute of the American West, Howe Brothers, 1986.
——. "Stride Toward Freedom: The Relocation of Indians to Cities, 1952–1960." *Western Historical Quarterly* 16 (1985): 175–90.
Pool, Ian. *Te Iwi Maori: A New Zealand Population, Past, Present and Projected*. Auckland: Auckland University Press, 1991.
Prucha, Francis Paul. *The Great Father: The United States Government and the American Indians*. Abridged ed. Lincoln: University of Nebraska Press, 1986.
Putney, Diane Therese. "Fighting the Scourge: American Indian Morbidity and Federal Policy, 1897–1928." Ph.D. diss., Marquette University, 1980.
Ramenofsky, Ann F. *Vectors of Death: The Archaeology of European Contact*. Albuquerque: University of New Mexico Press, 1987.

Reff, Daniel T. *Disease, Depopulation, and Culture Change in Northwestern New Spain, 1518–1764.* Salt Lake City: University of Utah Press, 1991.

Rhoades, Everett R., Anthony J. D'Angelo, and Ward B. Hurlburt. "The Indian Health Service Record of Achievement." *Public Health Reports* 102 (1987): 356–60.

Richter, Daniel K. *The Ordeal of the Longhouse: The Peoples of the Iroquois League in the Era of European Colonization.* Chapel Hill: University of North Carolina Press, 1992.

Rindfuss, Ronald R., and James A. Sweet. *Postwar Fertility Trends and Differentials in the United States.* New York: Academic Press, 1977.

Ritzenthaler, Robert E. "Southwestern Chippewa." In *Northeast,* vol. 15 of *Handbook of North American Indians,* ed. Bruce G. Trigger, 743–59. Washington, D.C.: Smithsonian Institution, 1978.

Roessel, Ruth, ed. *Navajo Stories of the Long Walk Period.* Tsaile, Ariz.: Navajo Community College Press, 1973.

Romaniuk, A. "Increase in Natural Fertility During the Early Stages of Modernization: Canadian Indians Case Study." *Demography* 18 (1981): 157–72.

Rubinstein, Mitchell E., and Alan R. Woolworth. "The Dakota and Ojibway." In *They Chose Minnesota: A Survey of the State's Ethnic Groups,* ed. June Drenning Holmquist, 17–35. St. Paul: Minnesota Historical Society Press, 1981.

Ruby, Robert H., and John A. Brown. *Indians of the Pacific Northwest: A History.* Norman: University of Oklahoma Press, 1981.

Ruggles, Steven. "Comparability of the Public-Use Data Files of the U.S. Census of Population." *Social Science History* 15 (1991): 123–58.

———. "The Demography of the Unrelated Individual, 1900–1950." *Demography* 25 (1988): 521–36.

Salmon, Roberto Mario. "The Disease Complaint at Bosque Redondo (1864–68)." *The Indian Historian* 9 (1976): 2–7.

Sandefur, Gary D. "American Indian Migration and Economic Opportunities." *International Migration Review* 20 (1986): 55–86.

Sandefur, Gary D., and Trudy McKinnell. "American Indian Intermarriage." *Social Science Research* 15 (1986): 347–71.

Sandefur, Gary D., and Arthur Sakamoto. "American Indian Household Structure and Income." *Demography* 25 (1988): 71–80.

Sandefur, Gary D., and Wilbur J. Scott. "Minority Group Status and the Wages of Indian and Black Males." *Social Science Research* 12 (1983): 44–68.

Schoolcraft, Henry R. *Notes on the Iroquois; or Contributions to American History, Antiquities, and General Ethnology.* Albany, N.Y.: Erastus H. Pease and Co., 1847.

Schuster, Helen H. "Yakima Indian Traditionalism: A Study in Continuity and Change." Ph.D. diss., University of Washington, 1975.

———. *The Yakimas: A Critical Bibliography.* Bloomington: Indiana University Press, 1982.

Seaver, James E. *A Narrative of the Life of Mrs. Mary Jemison: White Woman of the Genessee.* 20th ed., revised by Charles Delamater Vail, New York: American Scenic and Historic Preservation Society, 1918.

Seneca Nation Constitution. In National Archives, *Correspondence of the Office of Indian Affairs (Central Office) and Related Records. Letters Received, 1824–1881.* M234, reel 573.

Shoemaker, Nancy. "The Census as Civilizer: American Indian Household Structure in the 1900 and 1910 U.S. Censuses." *Historical Methods* 25 (1992): 4–11.

———. "Demographic Indicators of American Indian Family Life in the Reservation Era." Paper presented at the annual meeting of the Organization of American Historians, Washington, D.C., March 1990.

———. "From Longhouse to Loghouse: Household Composition Among the Nineteenth-Century Senecas." *American Indian Quarterly* 15 (1991): 329–38.

———. "Urban Indians and Ethnic Choices: American Indian Organizations in Minneapolis, 1920–1950." *Western Historical Quarterly* 19 (1988): 431–47.

Shryock, Henry S., and Jacob S. Siegel. *The Methods and Materials of Demography.* Condensed ed. San Diego, Calif.: Academic Press, 1976.

Slocumb, John C., Stephen J. Kunitz, and C. L. Odoroff. "Complications with Use of IUD and Oral Contraceptives Among Navajo Women." *Public Health Reports* 94 (1979): 243–47.

Snaith, Linton M., and Tom Barns. "Fertility in Pelvic Tuberculosis: A Report on the Present Position." *The Lancet* 7 (1962): 712–16.

Snipp, C. Matthew. *American Indians: The First of This Land.* New York: Russell Sage Foundation, 1989.

———. "Who are American Indians? Some Observations About the Perils and Pitfalls of Data for Race and Ethnicity." *Population Research and Policy Review* 5 (1986): 237–52.

Snow, Dean R., and Kim M. Lanphear. "European Contact and Indian Depopulation in the Northeast: The Timing of the First Epidemics." *Ethnohistory* 35 (1988): 15–33.

Snow, Dean R., and William A. Starna. "Sixteenth-Century Depopulation: A View from the Mohawk Valley." *American Anthropologist* 91 (1989): 142–49.

Sorkin, Alan L. "Some Aspects of American Indian Migration." *Social Forces* 48 (1969): 243–50.

Stern, Bernhard J. "The Letters of Asher Wright to Lewis Henry Morgan." *American Anthropologist* 35 (1933): 138–45.

Stone, William L. *The Life and Times of Red-Jacket, or Sa-go-ye-wat-ha; Being the Sequel to the History of the Six Nations.* New York: Wiley and Putnam, 1841.

Strickland, Rennard. *Fire and the Spirits: Cherokee Law from Clan to Court.* Norman: University of Oklahoma Press, 1975.

Strong, Michael A., et al. *User's Guide: Public Use Sample: 1910 United States Census of Population.* Philadelphia: Population Studies Center, University of Pennsylvania, January 1989.

Stucki, Larry R. "The Case Against Population Control: The Probable Creation of the First American Indian State." *Human Organization* 30 (1971): 393–99.

Sturtevant, William C. "Oklahoma Seneca-Cayuga." In *Northeast,* vol. 15 of *Handbook of North American Indians,* ed. Bruce G. Trigger, 537–43. Washington, D.C.: Smithsonian Institution, 1978.

Svingen, Orlan J. "Jim Crow, Indian Style." *American Indian Quarterly* 11 (1987): 275–86.

Sweet, James A., and Larry L. Bumpass. *American Families and Households.* New York: Russell Sage Foundation, 1987.

Szasz, Margaret. *Education and the American Indian: The Road to Self-Determination, 1928–1973.* Albuquerque: University of New Mexico Press, 1974.

Tanner, Helen Hornbeck, ed. *Atlas of Great Lakes Indian History.* Norman: University of Oklahoma Press, 1987.

Thornton, Russell. *American Indian Holocaust and Survival: A Population History Since 1492.* Norman: University of Oklahoma Press, 1987.

———. "Cherokee Population Losses During the Trail of Tears: A New Perspective and a New Estimate." *Ethnohistory* 31 (1984): 289–300.

———. *The Cherokees: A Population History.* Lincoln: University of Nebraska Press, 1990.

Thornton, Russell, and Joan Marsh-Thornton. "Estimating Prehistoric American Indian Population Size for United States Area: Implications of the Nineteenth Century Population Decline and Nadir." *American Journal of Physical Anthropology* 55 (1981): 47–53.

Thornton, Russell, Tim Miller, and Jonathan Warren. "American Indian Population Recovery Following Smallpox Epidemics." *American Anthropologist* 93 (1991): 28–45.

Thornton, Russell, Gary D. Sandefur, and Harold G. Grasmick. *The Urbanization of American Indians: A Critical Bibliography.* Bloomington: Indiana University Press, 1982.

Thornton, Russell, Gary D. Sandefur, and C. Matthew Snipp. "A Research Note: American Indian Fertility Patterns: 1910 and 1940 to 1980." *American Indian Quarterly* 15 (1991): 359–67.

Tietze, Christopher. *The Effect of Breast-Feeding on the Rate of Conception.* New York: International Population Conference, 1961.

Tolnay, Stewart E., and Avery M. Guest. "American Family Building Strategies in 1900: Stopping or Spacing." *Demography* 21 (1984): 9–18.

Trafzer, Clifford E. *Death Stalks the Yakama: Epidemiological-Nutritional Transitions and Mortality on the Yakama Indian Reservation, 1888–1964.* East Lansing: Michigan State University Press, 1997.

Trennert, Robert A. *The Phoenix Indian School: Forced Assimilation in Arizona, 1891–1935.* Norman: University of Oklahoma Press, 1988.

Trigger, Bruce G. *The Children of Aataentsic: A History of the Huron People.* 2 vols. Montreal: McGill-Queen's University Press, 1976.

Trosper, Ronald L. "Native American Boundary Maintenance: The Flathead Indian Reservation, Montana, 1860–1970." *Ethnicity* 3 (1976): 256–74.

Ubelaker, Douglas H. "North American Indian Population Size, A.D. 1500 to 1985." *American Journal of Physical Anthropology* 77 (1988): 289–94.

———. "North American Indian Population Size: Changing Perspectives." In *Disease and Demography in the Americas*, ed. John W. Verano and Douglas H. Ubelaker, 169–76. Washington, D.C.: Smithsonian Institution, 1992.

———. "Prehistoric New World Population Size: Historical Review and Current Appraisal of North American Estimates." *American Journal of Physical Anthropology* 45 (1976): 661–66.

———. "Sources and Methodology for Mooney's Estimates of North American Indian Populations." In *The Native Population of the Americas in 1492*, ed. William M. Denevan, 243–88. Madison: University of Wisconsin Press, 1976.

Underhill, Ruth M. *The Navajos.* Norman: University of Oklahoma Press, 1956.

Unger, Steven. *The Destruction of American Indian Families.* New York: Association on American Indian Affairs, 1977.

United Nations, Population Division. Mortpak: The United Nations Software Packages for Mortality Measurement. Population Division, United Nations, 20 Sept. 1986.

U.S. Bureau of the Census. *1970 Census of Population: American Indians.* Washington, D.C.: GPO, 1973.

———. *1980 Census of Population: American Indians, Eskimos, and Aleuts on Identified*

Reservations and in the Historic Areas of Oklahoma (Excluding Urbanized Areas). Vol. 2, *Subject Reports*, pt. 2. Washington, D.C.: GPO, 1986.

———. *1980 Census of Population: Characteristics of the Population, United States Summary*. Vol. 1. Washington, D.C.: GPO, 1983.

———. *1980 Census of Population: United States Summary*. Vol. 1, ch. C, *General Social and Economic Characteristics*, pt. 1. Washington, D.C.: GPO, 1983.

———. *Census of Population, 1940 [United States]: Public Use Microdata Sample*. Ann Arbor, Mich.: Inter-University Consortium for Political and Social Research, 1984.

———. *Census of Population and Housing, 1980: Public Use Microdata Samples: Technical Documentation*. Washington, D.C.: GPO, 1983.

———. *Characteristics of American Indians by Tribes*. Washington, D.C.: GPO, 1980.

———. *Characteristics of the Population*. Washington, D.C.: GPO, 1943, 1953, 1964, 1973.

———. *Fifteenth Census of the United States: 1930. The Indian Population of the United States and Alaska*. Washington, D.C.: GPO, 1937.

———. *Historical Statistics of the United States: Colonial Times to 1970*. Pt. 1. Washington, D.C.: GPO, 1975.

———. *Indian Population of the United States and Alaska, 1910*. Washington, D.C.: GPO, 1915.

———. *Public Use Samples of Basic Records From the 1970 Census: Description and Technical Documentation*. Washington, D.C.: GPO, 1972.

———. *Sixteenth Census of the United States: 1940. Population: Characteristics of the Nonwhite Population By Race*. Washington, D.C.: GPO, 1943.

———. *Statistical Abstract of the United States, 1988*. Washington, D.C.: GPO, 1988.

———. *United States Census Data for 1960*. Ann Arbor, Mich.: Inter-University Consortium for Political and Social Research, January 1973.

———. *U.S. Census of Population: 1950. Nonwhite Population by Race*. Special report, vol. 14, pt. 3, chap. B. Washington, D.C.: GPO, 1953.

———. *U.S. Census of Population: 1960. Nonwhite Population By Race*. Washington, D.C.: GPO, 1961.

U.S. Census Office. *Extra Census Bulletin: The Five Civilized Tribes in Indian Territory*. Washington, D.C.: U.S. Census Printing Office, 1894.

———. *Indians Taxed and Indians Not Taxed in the United States (except Alaska) at the Eleventh Census: 1890*. Washington, D.C.: GPO, 1894.

U.S. Senate. Report of the Joint Special Committee on the Condition of the Indian Tribes. J. R. Doolittle, chairman. 39th Cong., 2d sess., 1867, S. Rept. 156.

U.S. Senate. *Tuberculosis Among the North American Indians: Report of a Committee of the National Tuberculosis Association Appointed on October 28, 1921*. Washington, D.C.: GPO, 1923.

Vecsey, Christopher, and William A. Starna, eds. *Iroquois Land Claims*. Syracuse, N.Y.: Syracuse University Press, 1988.

Verano, John W., and Douglas H. Ubelaker. *Disease and Demography in the Americas*. Washington, D.C.: Smithsonian Institution, 1992.

Wall, Jenny Bourne. "New Results on the Decline in Household Fertility in the United States from 1750 to 1900." In *Long-Term Factors in American Economic Growth*, ed. Stanley L. Engerman and Robert E. Gallman, 391–437. Chicago: University of Chicago Press, 1986.

Wallace, Anthony F. C. *The Death and Rebirth of the Seneca*. New York: Random House, 1969.

Wallach, E. E., A. E. Beer, and C.-R. Garcia. "Patient Acceptance of Oral Contraceptives, #1: The American Indian." *American Journal of Obstetrics and Gynecology* 97 (1967): 984–91.

Wardell, Morris L. *A Political History of the Cherokee Nation, 1838–1907*. Norman: University of Oklahoma Press, 1938.

Warren, William W. *History of the Ojibway People*. 1885. Reprint, St. Paul: Minnesota Historical Society Press, 1984.

Weber, Kenneth R. "Demographic Shifts in Eastern Montana Reservation Counties: An Emerging Native American Political Power Base?" *Journal of Ethnic Studies* 16 (1989): 101–16.

Weiss, Kenneth M. "Evolutionary Perspectives on Human Aging." In *Other Ways of Growing Old*, ed. Pamela T. Amoss and Stevan Harrell, 25–58. Stanford, Calif.: Stanford University Press, 1981.

Wheeler-Voegelin, Erminie, and Harold Hickerson. *The Red Lake and Pembina Chippewa*. Vol. 1 of *Chippewa Indians*. New York: Garland, 1974.

Wilkins, Thurman. *Cherokee Tragedy: The Story of the Ridge Family and the Decimation of a People*. New York: Macmillan, 1970.

Wilson, William Julius, and Kathryn M. Neckerman. "Poverty and Family Structure: The Working Gap Between Evidence and Public Policy Issues." In *Fighting Poverty: What Works and What Doesn't*, ed. Sheldon H. Danziger and Daniel H. Weinberg, 232–59. Cambridge, Mass.: Harvard University Press, 1986.

Witherspoon, Gary. *Navajo Kinship and Marriage*. Chicago: University of Chicago Press, 1975.

"Women of All Red Nations Respond to Official Government Report on Health Problems." *Lakota Times*, 18 Feb. 1982, 8.

Wood, Peter H. "The Changing Population of the Colonial South: An Overview by Race and Region, 1685–1790." In *Powhatan's Mantle: Indians in the Colonial Southeast*, ed. Peter H. Wood, Gregory A. Waselkov, and M. Thomas Hatley, 61–66. Lincoln: University of Nebraska Press, 1989.

Worcester, Donald E. *The Apaches: Eagles of the Southwest*. Norman: University of Oklahoma Press, 1979.

Wright, Muriel H. *A Guide to the Indian Tribes of Oklahoma*. Norman: University of Oklahoma Press, 1951.

Wrigley, E. A. and R. S. Schofield. *The Population History of England, 1541–1871: A Reconstruction*. London: Edward Arnold, 1981.

Yasuba, Yasukichi. *Birth Rates of the White Population in the United States, 1800–1860*. Baltimore, Md.: Johns Hopkins University Press, 1961.

Young, T. Kue. *Health Care and Cultural Change: The Indian Experience in the Central Subarctic*. Toronto: University of Toronto Press, 1988.

INDEX

Mooney, James, 2, 21

mortality, 8; in 1900, 39-41, 40(t); bias in estimates of, 40; changes in, 8, 13; comparison of white, black, and Indian, 9; and Long Walk, 33; lowering of, by intermarriage, 64; and modernization, 57; of Navajos, 33, 35; questions asked women used to gauge, 39; rates of, 10; relationship between fertility and, 44

Moses, Chief, 31

multiple classification analysis, 93; for 1960, 94(t); for 1970, 95(t); for 1980, 96(t)

nadir estimates, 2

Nag, Moni, 65

natural fertility, 48

natural increase, 7

Navajo Reservation, 16, 32; growth of, 34

Navajos, 32-35; and accumulation of wealth, 67; and childlessness, 52(t); and child-spacing, 53(t); dispersed residence pattern of, 66; economy of, 67, 67; estimated pre-Columbian population size, 32; and fertility, 42(t), 43(t), 50(g), 59(t); and households, 70(t), 72(t); and intermarriage, 63(t); as largest tribe, 32; literacy of, 61(t); and marital status, 46(t); and mortality, 35, 40(t); never-married women among, 46(t); "outfits," 70; and population increase, 37(t); population of, 1867-1980, 33(t), 34(g); as powerful Indian tribe, 32; pre-Civil War population size estimate for, 32; and raising livestock, 34; reasons for growth of, unclear, 35; and removal, 36; and school attendance, 62(t); size of, before European contact, 32; and slave trade, 32; and starting and stopping childbearing, 51(t); and tuberculosis, 54

Neosho Agency, 18

New York State Indians, 11

nonindustrial societies, fertility behavior in, 44

nuclear-family households, and fertility, 69

occupations, 58

Ojibways, 25-28; and epidemics, 28; migration to Red Lake area, 25; and movement to White Earth Reservation, 28; warfare with Dakotas, 25; westward migration of, 25. See also Red Lake Ojibways

Oklahoma, 23, 24, 65; child-woman ratio in, 12-13; infant mortality in, 10

Omran, Abdel, 35

overreporting, 16

own-children, 41–43, 50, 90

Paiutes, 32; and movement to Yakama Reservation, 31

Palouses, 31

Peru, population recovery in, 2

Pestilence and Famine, Age of, 35

polygamy, 47-48; elimination of, in Cherokee Nation, 48; among Navajos, 48; reluctance to admit to, 123n. 15

population: changing composition of, 8; of Cherokees, 1721-1980, 22(t); contradictory count of, 16; decline of, accompanies European influx, 1-2; decline of, and American Revolution, 17; difficulty in obtaining reliable information about, 1; enumerated versus projected, 7(g); estimates for pre-Columbian, 1-2; estimates range widely in size of, 3; increases in, per tribe, 37(t); inflated count of, 16, 31; nadir point of, 3; of native Americans, in the U.S., 1850-1990, 4(t); of Navajos, 33(t); problems in determining size of, 15; range in estimated count of Indian, 2; of Red Lake Ojibways, 1805-1980, 26(t); of Senecas, 1771-1980, 18(t); surges in, 7; and unreliability of count, 3; various methods used to aggregate totals of, 15; of Yakamas, 1805-1980, 29(t)

population growth: reasons for, 5, 8; of Senecas, 20

population recovery: as a multi-stage process, 99; beginning of, 3; lack of single cause for, 62